REAL
MARRIAGE

THE TRUTH ABOUT SEX, FRIENDSHIP, & LIFE TOGETHER

PARTICIPANT'S GUIDE

BY MARK AND GRACE DRISCOLL
WITH BRAD HOUSE

THOMAS NELSON
Since 1798

NASHVILLE   DALLAS   MEXICO CITY   RIO DE JANEIRO

Published in Nashville, Tennessee, by Thomas Nelson. Thomas Nelson is a
registered trademark of Thomas Nelson, Inc.

Published in association with Yates & Yates, LLP, www.yates2.com

Thomas Nelson, Inc., titles may be purchased in bulk for educational,
business, fund-raising, or sales promotional use. For information, please e-mail
SpecialMarkets@ThomasNelson.com.

Scripture taken from The New King James Version®. Copyright © 1982 by
Thomas Nelson, Inc. Used by permission. All rights reserved.

ISBN: 978-1-4185-5042-4

Printed in the United States of America

11 12 13 14 QG 6 5 4 3 2

CONTENTS

HOW TO USE THIS GUIDE

This study has been designed to help you and your community experience the transforming power of the gospel within your marriages. It is a companion to the book by Mark and Grace Driscoll, *Real Marriage: The Truth about Sex, Friendship, and Life Together*. This guide corresponds with each chapter of the book and will help you put its truths into practice in your own marriage. Reading the corresponding chapter before each session will greatly enhance your experience and will benefit your marriage. This guide will help you interact with your group and your spouse and provides space for you to keep notes and journal as you walk through the process.

GROUP GATHERINGS: Review the introduction of each session before you meet to reacquaint yourself with the material and to prepare for the discussion. Each group session is designed to begin with your group leader summarizing the information in the introduction. The group will then watch a short video and read a Scripture reflection. Questions are provided each week to help you dig into the topics more deeply as a group. Some weeks you will meet all together as one group, and some weeks you will divide into two groups by gender to facilitate discussion on particular topics.

PRAYER: Each week's session has a list of topics to facilitate a time of group prayer. It is common for a group to leave little time for this, but we encourage you to make this a priority for your group. Taking your marriages to the foot of the cross may be your most fruitful time together.

HOMEWORK: Oh, yes, there is homework. Developing a real marriage is not going to happen by just talking about it with your friends. The homework is designed to be completed on your own after your group meets for that week's session. This participant's guide provides a "Reflect" section to guide personal contemplation for each session. There are specific "Reflect" sections for the husband, the wife, and singles. Set aside time each week to prepare your heart for discussing your marriage with your spouse. In the "Connect" section each week, you will interact as a couple to share what God has been doing in each of you and to consider what He wants to do within your marriage.

EXPERIENCE: The final section for each week provides details for planning an interactive experience for you and your spouse. Some experiences will require advance planning, so be sure to look ahead. Many can be done after work or after the kids have gone to bed. Make time for these experiences each week, as they are designed to enhance what you have been learning and will bless your marriage.

SINGLES: If you are single, you may be wondering if this study is for you. While the book and this study are intended primarily for married couples, there is plenty of value to those of us who are single. Each study has a "Reflect" session designed for singles which will help you wrestle through the material as preparation for marriage or simply to understand how these principles apply to your life. The "Experience" sections are also adapted for singles when appropriate.

SAFETY: The content of this study is very personal and will at times be fairly sensitive. We'd like to further clarify what it means for your group to be a safe place. We all know that the ability of our groups to be places for honest and authentic discussion depends a great deal on our level of trust in one another. We often talk about the need for a safe place to share what God is doing in our lives but we don't necessarily have a consistent definition of "safe."

What safe means:

1. We lead with grace. This means we respond to one another in light of what Christ has done for us, understanding that we are all in need of His grace, compassion, and mercy.

2. We listen before offering advice.

3. We are free to wrestle with ideas and even disagree without judgment, personal attack, or dismissal.

4. We do not gossip, not even through prayer.

What safe does not mean:

1. It does not mean we are safe to live in sin. Community should be a dangerous place for sin as we call one another to confession and repentance. We are not judgmental, but we will address sin in a way that encourages restoration and redemption.

2. It does not mean that we can avoid participation. Community is not a safe place to hide. It is a safe place to live out God's call on our lives.

As a community, your group needs to agree with one another that you are committed to providing a safe place to be challenged by the Word of God and to let Him do a healing, sanctifying work in your lives. If you don't feel safe in your group, tell your leader. Your group may need to talk through what it means to provide a safe environment before you can effectively work through this study. If your group leader is the source of your concern, let a pastor know and submit to his authority as he helps you work through the issues.

THE GOSPEL: This study relies heavily on submitting to God and His Word. Nothing in your marriage can change apart from the person and the work of Jesus Christ in your life and your marriage. The gospel, or good news, of what Jesus has done on your behalf for your salvation is the foundation of the Christian life. If you are working through this study and you have doubts about whether you are a Christian, speak with your small group leader or pastor about what Jesus has done for you and how you can become His disciple.

INTRODUCTION

You don't want Pastor Mark's marriage, and he doesn't want yours.

But what we all should want are marriages that glorify God and reflect the grace of our Lord Jesus.

As you go through this study, remember that the marriage you want has been paid for on the cross. Experiencing a life-giving marriage full of fun, depth, and transformation begins not by doing more, but by receiving the grace of God.

As you work through this study with your spouse and your community, I pray that you will do so with humility and submission to the Bible and the Holy Spirit.

God loves you and wants your marriage to be a source of blessing and joy. Trust Him with your life and marriage, and not only will you get the marriage you want, you will get the marriage you need.

—Brad House, pastor of community groups at Mars Hill Church

SESSION 1

NEW MARRIAGE, SAME SPOUSE

INTRODUCTION

Has your marriage been everything you expected and dreamt about on your wedding day?

For most of us, marriage has been a series of surprises and challenges we didn't expect on the day we cut the cake. Circumstances change, and people change. But God doesn't call us to find a new spouse when these unexpected things occur. Quite the opposite. Scripture uses the image of a vineyard, or a garden, to illustrate the potential beauty, joy, and fruitfulness of marriage. It also illustrates its fragility and need for tending to keep at bay the things that can rob it of all that potential. Those of you who are gardeners can appreciate the imagery—often the most beautiful and fruitful plants need the most care and maintenance. We need to keep this imagery in mind as we go through the next several weeks of this study.

The truth is healthy, joy-filled marriages don't just happen; we must contend for our marriages as couples and as a community. The goal of this curriculum is to produce God-honoring marriages full of joy and life that reflect the truth of the gospel. During the next eleven weeks we will wrestle with tough questions and topics that we often avoid but desperately need to address.

As couples, you will experience a new vitality in your marriage with a renewed passion for each other and appreciation for what Jesus has done for your marriage. But experiencing a new marriage with your spouse will require humility, repentance, forgiveness, and a dependence on God. If you can commit to these things, you will be well on your way to experiencing real marriage.

You may be in a group of people that just met for the first time or in a group that has been together for years. Either way, you will spend some time getting to know one another better. If you have been together for some time, don't assume you know each other as well as you think. Take time to pursue one another and be prepared to learn something new. Before your first group session, read chapter 1 of the book.

WATCH VIDEO: REAL MARRIAGE
VIDEO 1: NEW MARRIAGE, SAME SPOUSE

VIDEO RESPONSE

1. How long have you been married?

2. What is your favorite memory from your wedding day?

SCRIPTURE REFLECTION

Ephesians 5:21–33 is often quoted in Christian marriage ceremonies. With this in mind, let us take some time to read through the foundation for Ephesians 5:22–33, which starts in the previous chapter.

Ephesians 4:20–24

> But you have not learned Christ, if indeed you have heard Him and have been taught by Him, as the truth is in Jesus: that you put off, concerning your former conduct, the old man which grows corrupt according to the deceitful lusts, and be renewed in the spirit of your mind, and that you put on the new man which was created according to God, in true righteousness and holiness.

REFLECT: In what way does this lay the foundation for Ephesians 5? How does this change the way you read those verses?

GROUP DISCUSSION

In our discussion today, we want to start by laying some ground rules for the group since we will discuss some sensitive topics in the coming weeks. To reach the goals we have set for the next eleven weeks, we need to be committed to allowing the gospel to renew our minds, and we need to be able to count on one another to speak the gospel into our lives. It goes without saying that there is an expectation of discretion regarding our conversations within the group. That means no gossip, including not using prayer as a way to disclose the struggles of others. There is also an expectation that we come with a determination to submit our lives and marriages to the Bible and the kingship of Jesus. By committing to this study for the next eleven weeks, you are inviting the other members of this group to call you out if you are not participating in the group discussion or doing your homework. Obviously this should be done in love out of a desire to see transformation in one another's lives rather than out of duty, arrogance, or adherence to rules.

Today, we will also discuss the assumptions and expectations that we brought into our marriages to see what impact they have had on our marriages. Our goal over the course of this study is to align our expectations with those established by God. As we realign our expectations, we are preparing our hearts and minds for God to breathe new life into our marriages.

GROUP QUESTIONS

1. What expectations do we need to address within our small group to ensure that we can be transparent with one another and depend on one another as we work together toward healthier marriages?

2. What are we each hoping to get out of this study? What brought you here?

3. How do assumptions and expectations affect our marriages (especially when they are unspoken)?

4. What are the sources of our expectations? How does the origin of our expectations impact the effect they have?

5. How does our view of God affect our trust in His expectations for our marriage?

6. As we talk about a new marriage with the same spouse, what does Ephesians 4:20–24 reveal about the key to a real marriage?

7. Paul uses regeneration (the re-creation of the believer in Christ) as a backdrop for the expectations for marriage. How then is marriage a proclamation of the gospel? How are we doing in proclaiming it?

PRAYER

- As we begin this journey together, pray for new marriages (with the same spouses) that glorify the gift-giver, our Father in heaven. Recognize the gift that marriage is and thank Him for the spouse you have been given.

- Pray as well that the Holy Spirit would be evident in our community and that we would grow in our ability to encourage one another and contend for our marriages.

- Lastly, pray that we would set God's expectations for our marriages and that the gospel would be reflected clearly and accurately in the way we love our spouses.

HOMEWORK
INTRODUCTION

The goal of this week's homework is to reflect more specifically on assumptions and expectations and how they can affect your marriage. Unspoken expectations can cause bitterness and frustration. Take time to prayerfully think through the questions and prepare to share with your spouse. The exercises this week should help you pursue each other and align your vision and expectations for your marriage.

REFLECT: HUSBAND

1. Write down the assumptions you made going into your marriage.

2. How has the reality of your marriage challenged these assumptions?

3. How might God be using these challenges to make you a better husband?

4. Write down the expectations that you had going into your marriage.

5. How many of the expectations that you had were of yourself, and how many were of your wife? What does that reveal?

6. What are you praying God will do throughout the next eleven weeks?

7. Think and pray through your own life story, especially your life before marriage and your life before Jesus. (If you are not sure you have ever submitted your life to Jesus, take time now to talk to your small group leader or pastor.) Think through ideas and experiences that may have a significant effect on your marriage, such as your relationship with your father and mother, your parents' relationship, your previous relationships/experiences, your religious experiences, and so on, and prepare your story so you can share it with your wife. Don't assume that she already knows all of it, and don't assume you have anything in your story that she doesn't need to hear.

8. At some point this week, read chapter 2 in the book.

REFLECT: WIFE

1. Write down the assumptions you made going into your marriage.

2. How has the reality of your marriage challenged these assumptions?

3. How might God be using these challenges to make you a better wife?

4. Write down the expectations that you had going into your marriage.

5. How many of the expectations that you had were of yourself, and how many were of your husband? What does that reveal?

6. What are you praying God will do throughout the next eleven weeks?

7. Think and pray through your own life story, especially your life before marriage and your life before Jesus. (If you are not sure you have ever submitted your life to Jesus, take time now to talk to your small group leader or pastor.) Think through ideas and experiences that may have a significant effect on your marriage, such as your relationship with your father and mother, your parents' relationship, your previous relationships/experiences, your religious experiences, and so on, and prepare your story so you can share it with your husband. Don't assume that he already knows all of it, and don't assume you have anything in your story that he doesn't need to hear.

8. At some point this week, read chapter 2 in the book.

CONNECT

Discuss the following questions together as a couple.

1. What is the Holy Spirit revealing to you about your assumptions and expectations for your marriage?

2. Discuss what effects those expectations and assumptions have had on your marriage. How can you align them with the expectations that we see in Ephesians 4?

3. Share with each other your hopes for the next eleven weeks and write them down.

4. Take turns sharing your stories with each other. Listen specifically for the elements of the gospel in your spouse's story, either the truth of the gospel or the distortion of it. Help each other see what God has redeemed and what He wants to redeem in each of your stories.

5. Work together to come up with a vision statement for your marriage and family that is inspired by the gospel, glorifies Jesus, and gets you excited for the next twenty years of your life together.

REFLECT: SINGLE

1. Write down the assumptions you have about marriage.

2. How has hearing about real marriage in the first chapter of the book and in your group discussion challenged these assumptions?

3. How might God be using these challenges to prepare you for marriage and encourage you in your singleness?

4. Write down your expectations for marriage.

5. How many of these expectations are of yourself, and how many are of your future spouse? What does that reveal?

6. What are you praying God will do throughout the next eleven weeks?

7. Pray through your own life story, especially your life before Jesus. (If you are not sure you have ever submitted your life to Jesus, take time now to talk to your small group leader or pastor.) Think through ideas and experiences that may have a significant effect on your future marriage, such as your relationship with your father and mother, your parents' relationship, your previous relationships/ experiences, your religious experiences, and so on, and prepare your story so you can share it with a trusted friend or your future spouse.

8. At some point this week, read chapter 2 in the book.

EXPERIENCE

In the weeks to come, this section will outline experiences that you will share together to take what you have been learning and put some flesh on it. This will help galvanize the work the Holy Spirit has been doing throughout the week, and at the very least, get you some alone time together. This week will be more about preparation for those coming experiences. Some experiences will require time out of the house, meaning you may need a babysitter or possibly to make other arrangements in order for the experience to happen. With this in mind, take a look at the list below and talk through what arrangements need to be made in preparation for the upcoming weeks. Don't wait until the last minute! Weeks with asterisks require time out of the house. Others can be done outside of the house but do not require it. (Husbands, this is your opportunity to get things started on the right foot—take it.)

Week 1: Planning
Week 2: Date Night*
Week 3: Dinner and Questions
Week 4: Letters
Week 5: Taking Out the Trash
Week 6: Date Night*
Week 7: Washing with the Word
Week 8: Prayer
Week 9: Celebrate Your Spouse*
Week 10: Date Night at Home
Week 11: Reverse Engineering Getaway*

*These experiences may require the most advance planning since you will be away from home.

SINGLES: These experience times will offer great opportunities to offer your babysitting services for couples in your group or church. Your offer might be accepted more readily if you are well-known to the family and if you and a friend babysit together. Don't be offended if parents decline, but this could be a great blessing for some families.

FRIEND WITH BENEFITS

INTRODUCTION

The most important human friendship you have is the one with your spouse. Even if your marriage does not endure into eternity, your friendship will. Friendship is the one aspect of the marriage relationship that we can be certain we will take with us into eternity; in heaven, we will still hang out together as friends and recall our life together on earth, building new memories together in the kingdom of God.

Marriage starts out as a journey between friends, but often that journey gets off track. The key to a healthy marriage is to always be working on the friendship. Because, in the end, the rest of marriage seems to come together more easily and happily when you are working on it with your friend.

By living the life we should have lived, dying the death we should have died, and rising from the grave and conquering sin and death, Jesus made it possible for you and your spouse to be lifelong FRIENDS.

Fruitful: Friendship with one's spouse, like everything else, exists to glorify God and serve His kingdom.

Reciprocal: When both spouses make a deep heartfelt covenant with God to continually seek to become a better friend, the marriage is marked by increasing love and longing within both spouses.

Intimate: Deep friendships get beyond facts and opinions to the sharing of how we truly feel. Lifelong friends need to be transparent and vulnerable with each other.

Enjoyable: A friendship with an enjoyable spouse can make a world of difference. Any couple that hopes to exit this life still holding hands must be friends who have fun along the way.

Needed: We need human friendships in addition to friendship with God. The more a husband's need for his wife and a wife's need for her husband are celebrated as gracious gifts from God, the more oneness and friendship blossom in the marriage.

Devoted: Proverbs 17:17 says, "A friend loves at all times, and a brother is born for adversity." In marriage, being a devoted friend in all of life's seasons is essential to building oneness, intimacy, and trust.

Sanctifying: As sanctifying friends, a married couple needs to lovingly, humbly, graciously, and kindly speak the truth in love to each other so that they may each grow to be more like Jesus Christ.

REVIEW: Share with the group how God has used your conversations regarding expectations last week and what you learned from sharing your stories with one another during your reflection time as a couple.

WATCH VIDEO: REAL MARRIAGE
VIDEO 2: FRIEND WITH BENEFITS

VIDEO RESPONSE

Why are friendships so important to a healthy marriage?

SCRIPTURE REFLECTION

Our American culture often puts marriage, friends, and sex into three separate and mutually exclusive categories, but the Bible does not. Read from Song of Solomon 5:10–16 and see how the Bible puts them together.

Song of Solomon 5:16

His mouth is most sweet,
Yes, he is altogether lovely.
This is my beloved,
And this is my friend,
O daughters of Jerusalem!

GROUP DISCUSSION

Today's discussion will focus on what it means to be friends with our spouses. Friendship provides a foundation for a lasting relationship and is vital to a healthy marriage. We need to be honest with one another regarding the state of our friendship; and if we are struggling, we need to be willing to receive help from one another. Friendship, like our marriages, is a gift from God to be nurtured, celebrated, and enjoyed. Help one another see the value of this gift from our loving Father.

GROUP QUESTIONS

1. Is the importance of friendship in your marriage a new concept for you? Explain why or why not.

2. Which of the seven attributes of friendship (see the FRIENDS acrostic) most resonates with you, and with which do you have the hardest time identifying? Talk through why that might be the case.

3. How can we, as a community, help one another be better friends without being condemning and without enabling unhealthy relationships?

4. How does the Bible's view of marriage, sex, and friendship contrast with that of our culture?

5. How does seeing marriage as God's tool to make you and your spouse holy change the way you would approach your marriage?

6. How does the gospel make friendship with your spouse possible?

7. What will it look like for you to receive the grace of God and pursue friendship with your spouse as a response to what Jesus has done, rather than pursuing that friendship out of duty?

PRAYER

• This week, begin prayer by thanking Jesus for making friendships possible and designing us to be and need friends.

• Pray that we as couples would be honest with one another regarding the state of our friendships.

• Finally, pray that our friendships with our spouses would grow in a way that would honor Christ and fill us with joy.

HOMEWORK
INTRODUCTION

This week you are going to take an honest look at the state of your friendship with your spouse. Be honest about the areas you feel are lacking and about the areas you feel are going well. This is not a time to criticize or blame your spouse for deficiencies but an opportunity to identify areas in which you can grow as a couple.

REFLECT: HUSBAND

1. Using the FRIENDS acrostic of attributes of friendship, rate on a scale of 1 to 10 (1 is lowest, 10 is highest) how you are doing at being a friend to your wife.

   Fruitful

   Reciprocal

   Intimate

   Enjoyable

   Needed

   Devoted

   Sanctifying

2. Overall, how would you describe your friendship with your wife?

3. What areas of friendship are you most concerned about in your marriage?

4. What can you start doing to be a better friend? Write down three areas you want to focus on over the next two months.

5. Are you pursuing other friendships more diligently than the friendship with your wife? If so, write down why you think that is the case.

6. In what ways could your wife pursue you as a friend more effectively than she is now?

7. At some point this week, read chapter 3 in the book.

REFLECT: WIFE

1. Using the FRIENDS acrostic of attributes of friendship, rate on a scale of 1 to 10 (1 is lowest, 10 is highest) how you are doing at being a friend to your husband.
   Fruitful
   Reciprocal
   Intimate
   Enjoyable
   Needed
   Devoted
   Sanctifying

2. Overall, how would you describe your friendship with your husband?

3. What areas of friendship are you most concerned about in your marriage?

4. What can you start doing to be a better friend? Write down three areas you want to focus on over the next two months.

5. Are you pursuing other friendships more diligently than the friendship with your husband? If so, write down why you think that is the case.

6. In what ways could your husband pursue you as a friend more effectively than he is now?

7. At some point this week, read chapter 3 in the book.

CONNECT

1. Share your ratings of the seven FRIENDS attributes, and give your marriage an average score for each.

2. What jumps out at you? Discuss which areas are challenges in your friendship right now.

3. Share with each other your overall satisfaction with the friendship in your marriage. Is there unity in your satisfaction? What can you each start doing to increase that satisfaction?

4. How can you as a couple receive the gospel in such a way that it breathes new life into your friendship?

5. Rework the vision statement for your marriage (created in step 5 of last week's Connect time), incorporating what you have learned this week about friendship.

REFLECT: SINGLE

1. Using the FRIENDS acrostic of attributes of friendship, rate on a scale of 1 to 10 (1 is lowest, 10 is highest) how you are doing at being a friend to others.
Fruitful
Reciprocal
Intimate
Enjoyable
Needed
Devoted
Sanctifying

2. Overall, how would you rate the quality of your friendships?

3. How might your tendencies as a friend affect your potential future marriage?

4. What can you start doing to be a better friend? Write down three areas you want to focus on over the next two months.

5. At some point this week, read chapter 3 in the book.

EXPERIENCE

This week you are going to go out on a date night. In light of your discussion on friendship, this date is all about having fun. What is it that you love to do but haven't done for a while? Think of something you used to do when you were dating or something you always wanted to do together but haven't tried. The goal is to have fun together as friends. This is required homework—be prepared to share about your date with your group next week!

SINGLES: This is your first opportunity to offer your babysitting services for couples in your group or church. Your offer might be accepted more readily if you are well-known to the family and if you and a friend babysit together. Don't be offended if parents decline, but this could be a great blessing for some families.

SESSION 3

MEN AND MARRIAGE

INTRODUCTION

What does it mean to be a man? Is it about the car you drive, the job you have, or the clothes you wear? Is it about having freedom? Is it about instilling fear?

Paul said, "When I was a child, I spoke as a child, I understood as a child, I thought as a child ; but when I became a man, I put away childish things" (1 Corinthians 13:11). The world is in desperate need of men—real men. And no one feels that need more acutely than your wife. Ignoring problems while you watch the game won't change your marriage. Working longer hours at work won't change your marriage. Barking orders from your couch won't change your marriage. You have a God-given privilege to humbly and sacrificially lead your family, to love your wife, and to nurture your marriage. But on your own, you are incapable of being that man. That is where the good news is so good.

Jesus humbled Himself to be the man you should be. He sacrificed the life that you forfeited, and He rose from the dead so that sin and death would no longer have dominion over your life. When you submit your life to Him—truly submit and let go of back-up plans and foolish idols—He gives you everything you need to lead and nurture your wife as a reflection of the love you receive from Him.

But as men, we constantly swing between the extremes of pride. On one side is the pride of not needing help and the illusion that we are in control. On the other side is the pride of believing we deserve help and someone else should carry our burdens. Both extremes are childish. Real men understand their dependence on Christ and His provision of their needs. Real men understand that God has given them a great privilege and responsibility to reflect the image of Jesus to their wives.

When you hold the two in tension—dependence and responsibility—you *will* change your marriage through grace and for the glory of God. Not only did Jesus make this possible through the cross, He lived it out as an example for us. Jesus demonstrated the love that we can have for our wives by His sacrificial love for the church. He humbly set aside His divine privileges to become our sacrifice, not demanding His rights to headship but accepting the responsibility of headship with a dependence on the Holy Spirit to glorify His Father.

REVIEW: What has God been teaching you this past week about being a friend to your spouse? Share what you did on your date night last week.

WATCH VIDEO: REAL MARRIAGE
VIDEO 3: MEN AND MARRIAGE

VIDEO RESPONSE

In light of this chapter and the video, how would you expand your view of what it means to be childish?

SCRIPTURE REFLECTION

Paul makes it clear what it is to be a man in his first letter to the Corinthians: a real man puts away childish things and seeks after the things of God. If you want to be a righteous husband, it is time to follow the example of Jesus and accept the responsibility of being a man.

1 Corinthians 13:11

> When I was a child, I spoke as a child, I understood as a child, I thought as a child; but when I became a man, I put away childish things.

GROUP DISCUSSION

We are going to change things up a bit this week and have the men and women meet separately. This will allow for a more frank conversation and let men get down to business. If you haven't already broken into two groups, this would be a great time to do that. (If one group must go to the garage, I expect it to be the men.)

Men:

Take this opportunity to be real with your brothers. Today we will be evaluating how we are doing at being men and husbands. This is a time to boldly speak the gospel into one another's lives and call one another to lead our families in a way that glorifies Christ.

MEN'S GROUP QUESTIONS

1. In what areas of your life do you feel you have given in to the cultural norm of extended adolescence?

2. Of the eight characters of a man pictured in this chapter in the book, which best describes you as a husband? (LEADER: go over the eight characters of a man in chapter 3 of the book as a refresher.)

3. In what ways are you not honoring your wife physically, emotionally, verbally, financially, or technologically?

4. In what ways is God calling you to repent of childish behavior and accept the gift and responsibility of being a man?

5. How are you leading your family spiritually? (Church, Theology, and Home as discussed in chapter 3 of *Real Marriage*)

6. How does your understanding of the gospel affect you as a husband?

7. What does it look like to respond to what Jesus has done rather than instill more rules in your life to become the husband your wife needs?

8. How can we encourage one another to lead our marriages to health?

Women:

Today we are going to talk about supporting our husbands as they wrestle through accepting the responsibility of being men. Be on guard with your own hearts, and do not use this time to criticize your husbands or allow one another to gossip (even about your own marriage). This should be a time to pray for and encourage your husbands.

WOMEN'S GROUP QUESTIONS

1. How can you encourage your husband and support him in leading your family?

2. What are some practical things you can do that can help clear the way for your husband to be more of a real man? Are there behaviors you have come to rely on that may be emasculating to him (for example: nagging, criticizing, manipulating, etc.)?

3. Why is it important for Jesus to be the center of hope for your marriage? Are you ever tempted to put all your hope in your husband instead of God?

4. In what ways do you struggle with trusting the goodness of God in this process?

5. How can we as women encourage one another to receive the gospel and find hope (and even joy) in the work the Holy Spirit is doing in us, whether or not our husbands are leading our families well?

6. Spend a significant amount of your time praying as a group for your husbands and the conversations they are having right now.

PRAYER

- Pray this week for honest conversation between couples that will lead to life and not condemnation.

- Thank Jesus for being an example of what it means to be a man and making it possible for men to walk in His example.

- Pray as well that the men in your group would accept the responsibility of leading their homes and that the gospel would saturate your families, your church, and your city.

HOMEWORK
INTRODUCTION

This week we are going to focus on the husbands. As men, our hope is not in our own ability to be what God requires of us. Our hope is that although we fail, Jesus did not and He was a perfect husband in our place. This week is not about condemnation for husbands; rather it is an opportunity to accept the grace of God in our justification on the cross and our ability to grow through the help of the Holy Spirit. Men, engage in this conversation with your wife in humility and be committed to hear from her. Find your identity in what Christ has done, and you won't feel the need to save face. Make it safe for her to be honest with you, and let God use the conversation to shape you into the man He has made possible for you to be.

REFLECT: HUSBAND

1. Write down areas in which you believe God wants you to grow.

2. Write down specific steps you can start taking to address these areas in your marriage.

3. Write down specific ways God wants you to honor your wife physically, emotionally, verbally, financially, or technologically.

4. Write down a plan for how you are going to lead your family spiritually.

Home

Wife

Kids

Theologically

Church

Community

Service

Giving

5. Write down what you know of your wife:

Favorite food:

Favorite restaurant:

Favorite perfume:

Favorite book:

Favorite movie:

Favorite way to relax:

What makes her feel most loved:

Favorite memory:

Favorite thing to do on a date:

Dress size:

Ring size:

Favorite gift to receive:

Greatest fear:

Biggest struggle:

6. At some point this week, read chapter 4 in the book.

REFLECT: WIFE

1. Write down areas in which you would like to see you husband lead more in your family.

2. Describe how it would, or does, make you feel to see him lead in those areas.

3. What questions do you wish your husband would ask you? Make a list of those questions.

4. What do you most appreciate about your husband? How often do you share that with him? How do you think he would respond if you shared it more often?

5. At some point this week, read chapter 4 in the book.

CONNECT

1. Husbands, talk through the plan you made for leading the family. Wives, share areas of leadership you would like to add and share specifically what you wrote about how you feel when your husband leads.

2. Husbands, fill in any blanks you couldn't fill in about your wife during your Reflect time.

3. Wives, share the questions you wish your husband would ask you.

4. Talk through why those questions aren't being asked and how you can set aside time as a couple to ensure they do get asked in the future.

REFLECT: SINGLE

Men

1. What can you do now to grow up and be a man and prepare for being a husband and a father?

2. Write down specific areas in which you think you will have the hardest time honoring your future wife.

3. How can you address these issues today?

4. What does it look like to be a single man in contrast to a single boy?

5. At some point this week, read chapter 4 in the book.

Women

1. How has this study session changed what you are looking for in a husband?

2. Is your father exercising biblical headship in your life, looking out for you and filtering suitors? If not, how can you invite your community to be a covering for you?

3. How is Jesus that covering for you as well?

4. At some point this week, read chapter 4 in the book.

EXPERIENCE

For your exercise this week, we want you to think of a couple that has been married longer than you whose marriage you admire for its reflection of the gospel. (Pick someone other than your pastor and his wife, as they might be overwhelmed with requests.) Write down ten questions you would like to ask them about their marriage. Invite them to dinner at your house or at your favorite restaurant. Explain to them what their marriage has meant to the two of you, and ask your questions. Afterward, debrief on what you learned and how their answers might have surprised you.

SINGLES: This is a great experience for you as well. Invite a couple to dinner, or better yet, take them to a restaurant. Write down ten questions you would like to ask them about their marriage and discuss them over dinner. Afterward, write down the things you learned and want to remember for your future marriage.

SESSION 4

THE RESPECTFUL WIFE

INTRODUCTION

Respect.

Culturally, that can be a dirty word.

If the question of what it means to be a man is confused by our culture, understanding what it means to be a godly wife can be completely bewildering. We hear plenty of talk about respecting ourselves, but rarely, if ever, do we hear about respect for our husbands. And sometimes when we do hear about it, it is considered a joke or as condescending by equating a woman who has respect for her husband with being a doormat. True respect, however, is not demeaning, nor does it diminish you as a woman and an image bearer of God.

Even now, as you think of the idea of respect and submission, some of you may be squirming in your seats, uncomfortable with such concepts.

Your discomfort may be due to the fact that your husband is not the most respectable man. Maybe he is passive, disconnected, or overbearing.

The world tells us that we are justified in being disrespectful if our husband is not worthy of respect. The world calls such a response justified. The Bible calls it sin.

The truth is that our call to be wives who reflect the truth of the gospel is not dependent on the respectability of our husbands, just as our husbands' call to love us sacrificially is not dependent on our loveliness. Ephesians makes it clear when it says, "Let each one of you in particular so love his own wife as himself, and let the wife see that she respects her husband" (5:33). These are not "if-then" statements. These are commands that are not conditional.

This truth is a reflection of the gospel that God's grace is dependent not on our faithfulness but on the faithfulness of Jesus. We do well to be thankful for this because if our salvation was dependent on our righteousness, we would be condemned. So what right do we have to withhold grace and obedience to God based on the behaviors of our husbands?

If we rebel against the call to be a respectful wife, we are not rebelling against our husbands . . . we are rebelling against our God. If we want to experience a renewed marriage, we must allow God to define what it means for us to be a wife. We must find our identity in Christ and let our role as a wife be an expression of His image.

Being a wife is not a duty; it is a calling that through the power of the gospel can be life-giving and full of joy. Jesus is bigger than our fears. He understands them and provides us with the power to overcome them. This can happen, but it will start with your own heart. It begins with repentance and results in dependence. Will you give control of your marriage to God? Can you trust Him? Will you submit your life to Him?

The goal is not to fix our husbands or even to save our marriages. The goal is to glorify God and trust Him as a loving Father who commands us to respect our husbands, not out of duty, but because it reflects the glory of His Son. When we live our lives to reflect that glory, we don't have to fight for control, respect, or autonomy. We can, by the help of the Holy Spirit, fight for unity and oneness that will not only glorify God but also bring us the greatest joy. In this, our attitudes toward our husbands will change as we embrace the gift of being a God-designed helper for him that we get to love, enjoy, and respect.

REVIEW: What was the coolest thing you learned during your dinner last week?

WATCH VIDEO: REAL MARRIAGE
VIDEO 4: THE RESPECTFUL WIFE

VIDEO RESPONSE

In what ways does a wife's respect for her husband reflect the functional and dysfunctional relationship between every Christian and God our Father?

SCRIPTURE REFLECTION

In week 1, we looked at the foundation of Ephesians 5, namely the person and work of Jesus Christ. Against this backdrop we take a look at the commands of Ephesians 5.

Ephesians 5:22–24

Wives, submit to your own husbands, as to the Lord. For the husband is head of the wife, as also Christ is head of the church; and He is the Savior of the body. Therefore, just as the church is subject to Christ, so let the wives be to their own husbands in everything.

GROUP DISCUSSION

We are going to meet separately again this week. If you haven't already broken into two groups, this would be a great time to do that.

Men:

While your wife is charged by God to respect you as her husband, that charge is made in light of the gospel expectation that you love her as Christ loved the church. Her obedience is not dependent on your respectability but neither is yours. In light of last week's discussion on being a man and a husband, continue your conversation on how you can encourage and support your wife in what God is doing in her life.

GROUP QUESTIONS

1. Respect is a gift of grace; it is not your right as a husband. What does that concept mean to you, and how does it change your view of respect and submission?

2. How is God prompting you to cultivate what God is doing in your wife?

3. In what ways can and should you take responsibility for the sin of your wife?

4. Spend a significant portion of your time praying for your wives and the conversations they are having right now.

Women:

Today's topic may elicit some strong emotion. Our goal today is to be honest with where we are, yet allow the truth of the gospel to redefine what it means to be a wife. God is a loving Father who wants the best for you. His expectations are not to burden you; rather, they are a guide to your greatest joy. Let's humbly walk together as Jesus removes our blinders and gives us the freedom to be the women He has called us to be.

GROUP QUESTIONS

1. How would you define respect?

2. When it comes to head, heart, and hands (as discussed in chapter 4 of *Real Marriage*), which area is the biggest struggle for you?

3. What baggage do you carry regarding the idea of being your husband's "helper"? How might God want to redeem your view of being a helper?

4. Our ability to submit and respect our husbands is often a reflection of our ability to submit to God and Scripture. What does your relationship with your husband say about your relationship with God?

5. What does that reveal about distortions you have in your view of God and the gospel?

6. Discuss how respect and submission are expressions of the gospel in our lives.

7. How does the cross provide freedom for you to disagree with, counsel, encourage, and submit to your husband respectfully?

8. How is respecting your husband a sign of strength and not a sign of weakness? How can we encourage one another as wives in this area?

PRAYER

- Pray that God would be glorified in your discussions with your spouses this week and that the wives in your group would be encouraged by what Jesus has done on their behalf.

- Pray for tenderhearted husbands that would nurture their wives and cultivate what God is doing in them.

- Pray that your relationships would proclaim the truth of the gospel.

HOMEWORK
INTRODUCTION

Just as we focused on the husbands last week, this week will focus on wives. This is a time for hope and encouragement for what the Holy Spirit is doing in our lives. This is not a place for shame. Jesus paid for our sin and has given us the freedom to glorify Him through the respect we show our husbands. Embrace what He has done and share with your husbands what you have learned. Men, remember what you learned last week and be tender and understanding with your wife. Let God work in her, and be the gospel to her.

REFLECT: HUSBAND

1. Write down some areas in which your wife could help you in your walk to be a godly man.

2. Reflect on areas you have made it difficult for her to be a good helper.

3. Make a list of things you appreciate about your wife. How often do you share those things with her? How do you think she would respond if you shared them more often?

4. At some point this week, read chapter 5 in the book.

REFLECT: WIFE

1. In what specific areas does the Holy Spirit want you to grow in helping, respecting, and submitting to your husband?

2. What fears do you have regarding submitting to your husband?

3. How has Jesus made provision for those fears? (Note: If you feel you are being abused physically, emotionally, verbally, or spiritually, you need to let your community group leader or a pastor know immediately. Respect and submission to your husband does not mean you must endure abuse.)

4. Write down questions you could ask your husband that would help you be a better helper.

5. At some point this week, read chapter 5 in the book.

CONNECT

1. Husbands, start your time together by sharing the list of things you appreciate about your wife.

2. Wives, share what God has been doing in your heart and tell your husband that you want to be a wife who "does him good and not evil all the days of her life"(Proverbs 31:12). Then, respectfully ask him ways you are doing this well and ways you can do this better,

and make note of his answers. Ask him how he needs you to be a helper. Use your list of questions when necessary.

3. Husbands, lay hands on your wife and pray for her.

REFLECT: SINGLE

Men

1. How did this lesson change what you are looking for in a wife?

2. In what areas do you think you will need the most help when you get married?

3. At some point this week, read chapter 5 in the book.

Women

1. How has this lesson challenged you as a single woman?

2. What fears do you have regarding submission to your future husband?

3. How has Jesus made provision for those fears?

4. What does it look like to walk in faith for those provisions today?

5. At some point this week, read chapter 5 in the book.

EXPERIENCE

This week you are going to take some time individually to reflect on the last four weeks and write letters to each other. This is not an email or a 140-character tweet, but a good, old-fashioned letter.

The letter should include:

1. What God has been teaching you.

2. Asking for forgiveness for areas in which you have sinned against him/her.

3. Why you are thankful for having him/her as your spouse.

4. The vision you are praying for your marriage to fulfill.

You will share these with each other in your Connect time next week.

SINGLES: You are going to do the same activity, but you are going to write a letter to your future spouse. Statistically, most of us will get married someday. This is an exercise to get you thinking about what God has in store and what He wants to prepare in you for the future.

The letter should include:

1. What God has been teaching you.

2. How you are praying for your future spouse.

3. The vision you are praying for your marriage to fulfill.

SESSION 5

TAKING OUT THE TRASH

INTRODUCTION

It is time to take out the trash.

Years of accumulating sins against one another that get ignored add up quickly. Those sins may have been from commission or omission, things we have done to one another or things we failed to do, and they have a way of collecting. Like trash, unaddressed sin chokes out life and damages friendships. There is no room in your marriage for trash.

Sin separates what God has brought together and made good. From the beginning, our response to sin is separation from one another and God. In the face of sin, we hide from God, and we turn on one another, just as Adam did to Eve with those blame-shifting words: "It was the woman You gave me" (see Genesis 3:12).

As couples, we need to understand that God has a real enemy, and that enemy wants to destroy our marriages. This is because a marriage that is saturated with the gospel and is lived out in humility and dependence on the Holy Spirit is a megaphone for the good news of Jesus. It preaches louder than words the reconciling and redeeming power of the gospel.

And so the enemy attacks.

Our greatest defense for such an attack is repentance and forgiveness. Over the past two weeks, we have explored the areas in which we are being called as husbands and wives to allow the gospel to penetrate our lives. By now, we all have areas in which the Holy Spirit has brought out conviction of sin. Today we respond to that conviction.

We respond by receiving the grace of God in our own lives, recognizing the need for a rescuer because we have rebelled against the God of the universe. We submit our lives to the King who has lived perfectly in our place and took on the punishment that we deserved, that we might be saved to worship Him. We live in the power of the Holy Spirit that has been given to us to help us lead lives that reflect the wonder, power, and grace of our Savior.

First John 1:9 says, "If we confess our sins, He is faithful and just to forgive us our sins and to cleanse us from all unrighteousness." Our marriages are in desperate need of cleansing. What do you need to confess? What do you need to forgive?

The promise is clear: confess our sin, and God is faithful to forgive and cleanse. This is the promise of grace. This is unmerited favor from the Creator of the world. As we receive forgiveness from our Father, He asks us to forgive one another; not because our spouse deserves it, but because we have been forgiven. God does not withhold grace from us; it is arrogant to think that we have the right to withhold forgiveness from those who seek it from us. Therefore, receive the gospel and let it change your marriage.

We have accumulated a lot of trash . . . it is time to take it to the curb.

REVIEW: How have you been challenged in your roles as husbands and wives over the last two weeks?

WATCH VIDEO: REAL MARRIAGE
VIDEO 5: TAKING OUT THE TRASH

VIDEO RESPONSE

How does it make you feel when you are able to do some major spring cleaning?

SCRIPTURE REFLECTION

As we look to take out the trash, we rest in the faithfulness and promise that has been secured on the cross.

1 John 1:5–10

> This is the message which we have heard from Him and declare to you, that God is light and in Him is no darkness at all. If we say that we have fellowship with Him, and walk in darkness, we lie and do not practice the truth. But if we walk in the light as He is in the light, we have fellowship with one another, and the blood of Jesus Christ His Son cleanses us from all sin. If we say that we have no sin, we deceive ourselves, and the truth is not in us. If we confess our sins, He is faithful and just to forgive us our sins and to cleanse us from all unrighteousness. If we say that we have not sinned, we make Him a liar, and His word is not in us.

GROUP DISCUSSION

Today we are talking about repentance and forgiveness. True repentance is a combination of three things.

One, repentance includes confession. In confession, we agree with God that we have sinned. Confession includes both our minds and mouths. Two, repentance includes contrition. In contrition, we feel what God feels about our sin. Contrition includes both our emotions and expressions. Our heart is affected, not just our words. Three, repentance includes change. In change, we stop sinning and start worshiping.

Change includes our will and works. Every married couple has to continually practice repentance of sin if they hope to have any loving, lasting life together.

GROUP QUESTIONS

1. Why are the following integral to true repentance:
   Confession?
   Contrition?
   Change?

2. Describe some of the times when you have felt contrition for your sin.

3. From the chapter in the book, what surprised you about the list of what repentance is not?

4. Why is forgiveness an essential part of our walks with Christ? What happens if we are unwilling to forgive?

5. How do we prevent bitterness from taking root in our marriages?

6. What does it look like to fight in God-glorifying ways, as discussed in chapter 5 of *Real Marriage*?

PRAYER

- Pray for honest confession, authentic contrition, and true repentance that does not look back.

- Pray for the ability to let the blood of Christ cover sin and free us to forgive one another.

- Pray that our responses to one another this week would be proclamations of the power of the cross and resurrection to others in our lives.

HOMEWORK
INTRODUCTION

This week is going to be heavy. It is time to take what we talked about in the group session time and make it personal. After your personal reflection time, make sure you have a quiet place together where you won't get interrupted for your Connect time.

REFLECT: HUSBAND

1. What issues in your marriage do you need to personally own and take responsibility for?

2. Are you bitter against your wife in any way?

3. Of what do you need to repent to your wife?

4. For what do you need to forgive your wife?

5. What is keeping you from forgiving her?

6. At some point this week, read chapter 6 in the book.

REFLECT: WIFE

1. What issues in your marriage do you need to personally own and take responsibility for?

2. Are you bitter against your husband in any way?

3. Of what do you need to repent to your husband?

4. For what do you need to forgive your husband?

5. What is keeping you from forgiving him?

6. At some point this week, read chapter 6 in the book.

CONNECT

1. Share the letters you wrote for each other last week.

2. Take turns naming specific sins you have committed against each other and asking for forgiveness. Practice saying the words "you are forgiven" to each other.

3. Discuss how you can have more God-glorying fights in the future.

4. Pray together for the healing power of the gospel to saturate your marriage.

REFLECT: SINGLE

1. Reflect on things in your life for which you need to repent and ask forgiveness.

2. Consider those whom you have not forgiven and spend time praying for them.

3. Make a list of people whom the Holy Spirit is prompting you to talk to and make plans to meet with them.

4. How has Jesus made repentance possible for you personally?

5. At some point this week, read chapter 6 in the book.

EXPERIENCE

This week has been heavy, so we want you to do something fun. Pop some popcorn and take out your old photo albums or wedding videos and spend an evening walking down memory lane, recalling your favorite memories. Take a picture together and add it to the album.

SINGLES: This week, ask your parents or a couple you respect if they would show you their albums or marriage videos and share their stories with you. Ask questions about how they resolve conflict and what repentance and forgiveness look like in their marriage.

SESSION 6

SEX: GROSS, GOD, OR GIFT?

INTRODUCTION

One of the areas most affected by sin in our marriages is sex.

Not only is intimacy one of the first things affected by the separating power of sin, it is also a relatively taboo topic to discuss, especially in the church. Culturally, we are not allowed to talk about it unless we degrade it to something vulgar or elevate it to a deity. But now that we have taken out the trash in our last session and begun to walk in repentance and forgiveness, we can turn our attention to redeeming the bedroom. That redemption begins with understanding the poles of deception. There are two primary distortions we generally have regarding sex: seeing it as a god and seeing it as gross.

When we make sex the ultimate thing, we have made it a god. When it becomes the center of our lives, the pursuit of our desires, the ground of our identity, and the source of our hope, it has become our god. Do you have to have sex in order to experience intimacy? Without sex, do you become angry, fearful, or depressed? Will you sin to experience sexual pleasure? Then it may be a god for you. This distortion is made more powerful because this view of sex is reinforced everywhere in the world around us. Sex sells . . . but we don't have to buy.

Your god is lying to you. There is no freedom, comfort, joy, pleasure, or life at the end of the path on which you are travelling. But it is not too late. You need to be honest, you need to tell the truth, you need to get help, and you need to turn around and run for your life.

The opposite distortion is seeing sex as gross. This view is often an overreaction to the worship of sex, but it can be perpetuated by bitterness as a result of a sexually frustrated marriage. In some cases it may also be intensified as a result of abuse. Regardless of the source, this distortion is no less an enemy of the truth. To view sex as gross is to deny what God has made good and to undermine a blessing that He has designed for oneness between you and your spouse. When we believe that sex is bad, dirty, or vulgar, we have exchanged the truth for a lie. We denounce what God has proclaimed good and sabotage the unity of our marriage.

Whether we lean toward seeing sex as god or gross, we need to be honest with one another and repent of a sinful view of sex in our marriages. We need to allow the truth of God's Word to renew our minds and redeem our understanding of intimacy and the marriage bed. Honest conversations, repentance, obedience to God, teachable spirits, and praying together against fear and for freedom all lead to healthy intimacy.

Sex is a gift from God. It is a gift to be stewarded, a gift to be guarded, a gift to be enjoyed, and a gift to be shared together for God's glory and our good.

REVIEW: How has God moved in your marriage since your time of confession, repentance, and forgiveness?

WATCH VIDEO: REAL MARRIAGE
VIDEO 6: SEX: GROSS, GOD, OR GIFT?

VIDEO RESPONSE

How nervous or uncomfortable does it make you to have a conversation about sex? Is it culturally acceptable, or is it frowned upon?

SCRIPTURE REFLECTION

As we enter into our discussion today on the ways our view of sex gets distorted, let's start by looking at how it was supposed to be:

Genesis 2:21–24

> And the Lord God caused a deep sleep to fall on Adam, and he slept; and He took one of his ribs, and closed up the flesh in its place. Then the rib which the Lord God had taken from man He made into a woman, and He brought her to the man.
> And Adam said:
> "This is now bone of my bones
> And flesh of my flesh;
> She shall be called Woman,
> Because she was taken out of Man."
> Therefore a man shall leave his father and mother and be joined to his wife, and they shall become one flesh.

GROUP DISCUSSION

We are going to be talking about how our views of sex get distorted and what it looks like to have a redeemed view of sex. These distortions, which are the result of sin, can have a devastating effect on our marriages. But, if we can understand what God intended for sex, we can redeem it in our marriages and move toward unity and health.

GROUP QUESTIONS

1. How does American culture at large reinforce the idea of sex as a god?

2. Have you ever perceived sex as gross? If so, when and why?

3. Which is the predominant view in our local culture? Why is that the dominant view? Has it ever been different?

4. What are indications that we might have a distorted view of sex?

5. Why does our view of sex have such a strong influence on our marriage?

6. How does having a redeemed view of sex as a gift from God refute the distortions of sex as god or gross?

7. Were you surprised by any of the six benefits of sex to the marriage from chapter 6 of *Real Marriage*? Why or why not?

PRAYER

- Pray for a healthy and redeemed view of sex.

- Pray for honesty between spouses that would bring redemption of their marriage bed as they speak honestly and openly about what is going on in their hearts.

- Pray that a redeemed view of sex would lead to closer friendships between spouses and renewed unity.

HOMEWORK
INTRODUCTION

Your topic this week will be sex. If this is awkward for you and your
spouse, discussing why that is the case would be a great way to start your
Connect time. Your goal is to honestly look at distortions you may have
as a couple that could be affecting the intimacy and unity you have as
husband and wife.

REFLECT: HUSBAND

1. Which of the distortions of sex do you tend toward: god or gross?

2. How does that manifest itself in your relationship with your wife?

3. How have you sinned against your wife because of your view of sex?

4. What does repentance look like in this area for you?

5. At some point this week, read chapter 7 in the book.

REFLECT: WIFE

1. Which of the distortions do you tend toward: god or gross?

2. How does that manifest itself in your relationship with your husband?

3. How have you sinned against your husband because of your view of sex?

4. What does repentance look like in this area for you?

5. At some point this week, read chapter 7 in the book.

CONNECT

1. Share your distortions with each other, and ask how your spouse has been affected by your view of sex.

2. Confess ways you have sinned against one another sexually, and walk through forgiving each other.

3. Share with each other what you hope your intimacy would look like if it were redeemed by the cross.

REFLECT: SINGLE

1. Which of the distorted views of sex are you prone to: god or gross?

2. How might that sin affect your future relationships?

3. What does repentance look like for you in your singleness?

4. What does it look like to have a healthy view of sex as a single person?

5. At some point this week, read chapter 7 in the book.

EXPERIENCE

It is time again for a date night. Husbands, a few weeks ago you made a list of your wife's favorite things. Plan a date night for your wife with as many of her favorite things as you can pack into one night (and afford). Use your time together to get to know more about each other and enjoy your friendship.

SINGLES: This is another opportunity to offer your babysitting services for couples in your group or church. Your offer might be accepted more readily if you are well-known to the family and work in pairs. Don't be offended if parents decline; this could be a great blessing for some families.

SESSION 7

DISGRACE
AND GRACE

INTRODUCTION

Sins that we commit against one another are not the only sins that can have a dramatic effect on our marriages. More than 1 in 4 women have been sexually abused. More than 1 in 6 men have been sexually assaulted.

Sexual abuse is far too common, but we rarely talk about it—especially in the church. Some in your group may have been abused or assaulted but have never told anyone, not even their spouse. That is how disgrace works. Disgrace destroys, causes pain, deforms, and wounds. It alienates and isolates. Disgrace silences and shuns. The evil of such abuse is that it attacks our identity. It demands that we identify ourselves as victims. It accuses us, making us think we deserved the abuse. It shames us into believing that we are not worthy of God's love. These are all lies—lies to keep us from walking in the light and the freedom that the cross offers. Lies designed to increase the distance between us and God, our spouse, and our community.

As a community, or as the spouse of an abuse victim, we must begin by listening, loving, and speaking the life-giving truth of the gospel to victims of abuse. We have a High Priest in Jesus who is able to sympathize with our weakness, one who is compassionate and merciful, one who is able to cleanse us from the defilement that has been forced upon us.

First John 1:7–9 says: "But if we walk in the light as He is in the light, we have fellowship with one another, and the blood of Jesus Christ His Son cleanses us from all sin. If we say we have no sin, we deceive ourselves, and the truth is not in us. If we confess our sins, He is faithful and just to forgive us our sins and to cleanse us from all unrighteousness." This cleansing extends to those of us who have been the victims of the sin of others. To our sense of disgrace, God restores, heals, and re-creates through grace. He re-creates by making us new in Him and giving us a new identity.

You are a child of God.

You are justified, holy, and blameless.

You have been redeemed and set free.

You have been chosen and are dearly loved.

You are clean, lovely, and forgiven.

This is the power of the cross.

If you have been abused, we want you to hear that you don't have to live in fear or denial anymore. The way to move from denial, isolation, and self-protection is to look honestly at the assault that has been done to you. Healing begins when the secret is disclosed and the shackles of silence are broken. This makes room for the gospel to take center stage in our lives. It makes room for us to receive the gift of grace that was purchased for us on the cross.

If you are the spouse of someone who has been abused, you have a tremendous opportunity to speak life and healing into this person you love. Don't be afraid of what you might hear. Pray for the strength and compassion to be an instrument of grace to your spouse. In the past couple of weeks we have been challenged to become the husbands and wives our spouses need. Today will be an opportunity to put that vision into practice.

REVIEW: How has addressing distortions in your view of intimacy affected your unity and ability to pursue each other as a couple?

WATCH VIDEO: REAL MARRIAGE
VIDEO 7: DISGRACE AND GRACE

VIDEO RESPONSE

Why do you think so few people talk about abuse when it is unfortunately so common in our society?

SCRIPTURE REFLECTION

As we discuss the effects of abuse on our lives, we want to remember the promises secured for us on the cross.

Philippians 4:4–9

Rejoice in the Lord always. Again I will say, rejoice! Let your gentleness be known to all men. The Lord is at hand. Be anxious for nothing, but in everything by prayer and supplication, with thanksgiving, let your requests be made known to God; and the peace of God, which surpasses all understanding, will guard your hearts and minds through Christ Jesus.

GROUP DISCUSSION

Our discussion today will be heavy and must be fully guided by the Holy Spirit. The environment of safety that you have encouraged over the past few weeks may provide the freedom for someone in your group to talk about his or her past abuse for the first time. Be ready to shift gears if necessary. Spend more time listening than you do offering advice. If you don't know what to say, pray. While you may feel like you're in over your head dealing with some issues, remember two things. First, you can ask for help. Second, as believers we know the gospel truth and can speak it to one another. Don't dismiss or deflect issues because they seem daunting. If God so chooses to drop a bomb in your group, rely on Him to help you navigate through it as a community of believers who have been changed by the cross.

GROUP QUESTIONS

1. How would you define shame?

2. What effect does shame have on your relationships?

3. What do you think keeps us from bringing issues of abuse into the light, especially in the church community?

4. How can we address those fears? How can we respond to victims of abuse in a way that brings life?

5. How does finding our identity in Christ address those fears?

6. How have you experienced the power of the gospel in healing the wounds of abuse and cleansing from shame? (See John 1:7–9)

7. How does dealing with the past free us to make our healing more about Jesus rather than ourselves?

PRAYER

- Pray for those who have been abused, especially those who haven't yet brought it into the light, that they would be comforted and healed by what Jesus has already accomplished on the cross.

- Pray for the husbands and wives who are just finding out about their spouse's past abuse, that they would respond in redeemed and life-giving ways.

- Pray for those who are in abusive relationships, that they would seek and find help, and that your group would be a community that comes alongside them in this time of need.

HOMEWORK
INTRODUCTION

Don't make assumptions this week. Ensure that you are providing a safe place for each other to be honest and vulnerable. This may take awhile, so make sure you have a quiet place to talk where you won't get interrupted. If you have been abused and have never revealed that to your spouse, it might be time to bring it into the light. Many victims of abuse minimalize what happened to them, thinking, *It isn't as bad as what happened to so-and-so.* But any abuse, no matter how minor it may seem, is abuse and it can affect each person differently. Believe the promise of Christ and trust Him. It is OK for the two of you to stumble painfully and awkwardly through this, but at least you are moving forward. The key is to take off the masks and remove the fig leaves so that you can experience a deeper sense of unity and intimacy.

REFLECT: HUSBAND

1. Do you have any incidents of abuse about which you have not told your wife? If so, why have you kept it from her?

2. Have you made your marriage a safe place for your wife to open up about past experiences? How can you make it safer?

3. Have you abused your wife in any way, spiritually, sexually, physically, emotionally, or verbally? (If so, you not only need to confess this to your wife, you need to get help from outside your home. Call your community group leader or pastor and submit to them as your

spiritual covering to build a plan to restore you and protect your wife.)

4. At some point this week, read chapter 8 in the book.

REFLECT: WIFE

1. Do you have any incidents of abuse about which you have not told your husband? If so, why have you kept it from him?

2. Do you feel your marriage is a safe place to be open and honest about your past experiences? How could it be made safer?

3. Have you abused or been abused by your husband in any way, spiritually, sexually, physically, emotionally, or verbally? (If so, call your community group leader or pastor and submit to them as your spiritual covering to build a plan to restore you and your husband and protect you from abuse.)

4. At some point this week, read chapter 8 in the book.

CONNECT

1. Start your time by praying for freedom and courage for one another to speak honestly and openly.

2. Share past experiences, no matter how minor they may seem, that you believe are affecting intimacy in your marriage.

3. Are there any things that your spouse is currently doing to increase the pain of past abuse? Discuss what you think could be done to bring healing in those areas.

REFLECT: SINGLE

1. Have you experienced any incidents of abuse that you have not told anyone about?

2. If so, who do you feel you could talk to? Is there a family member, friend, or pastor you can approach about it, and trust God by bringing it into the light?

3. Have you abused anyone in your past? (If so, call your community group leader or pastor and submit to them as your spiritual covering to build a plan to restore you and provide restitution to your victim.)

4. At some point this week, read chapter 8 in the book.

EXPERIENCE

Set aside a night this week to go to bed early. Clear your mind of all the things you have to get done and spend an hour reading Scripture together as a couple. You can pick a favorite book of the Bible, read through Psalms, or read through all the promises you can find. The goal in light of the heavy conversations you've had this week is to refresh each other through the washing of the Word.

SINGLES: Read through your favorite psalms, and take some time to write your own psalm to God.

THE PORN PATH

INTRODUCTION

Pornography is a marriage killer.

It destroys intimacy and trust and will ultimately destroy your marriage. It is not a surprise that divorce rates are continuing to rise in a culture that spends more money on porn than it does on professional basketball, football, and baseball combined. It is a cancer that continues to move toward acceptability in our culture while it quietly cripples our marriages. Freedom will come as we come clean and walk in the light. Don't justify it. Don't justify any of it. Don't believe the lie that casually looking at porn periodically is not bondage. Don't believe that because you only look at soft-core skin flicks or ogle women in music videos that you aren't one of "those guys." And don't think that as a woman you are unsusceptible to pornography—while it may come in different forms for women, porn is not just a man's problem.

First John 3:9 teaches that "Whoever has been born of God does not sin, for His seed remains in him; and he cannot sin, because he has been born of God." God not only sets the standard of what it looks like to walk in righteousness, He also provides the means in Jesus, through whom we can experience such freedom. Rather than live in fear of what your spouse or friends will think of you if you come clean about a porn problem, take hold of the grace of God and trust that your identity is secure in Christ. Jesus is bigger than your shame.

As we looked at last week, "if we walk in the light as He is in the light, we have fellowship with one another, and the blood of Jesus Christ His Son cleanses us from all sin. If we say that we have no sin, we deceive ourselves, and the truth is not in us. If we confess our sins, He is faithful and just to forgive us our sins and to cleanse us from all unrighteousness" (1 John 1:7–9).

This is the promise of the gospel.

For those of you who are in bondage to porn, start by bringing it into the light and asking for help. If you have tried unsuccessfully to break the bonds of porn in your life, you need to start with your heart.

You may hate the consequences of porn.

You may hate getting caught and the shame that it brings.

You may hate being enslaved to sin.

But inability to find freedom is an indication that you are still protecting the high you get from indulging in it. You won't experience freedom through the gospel if you are maintaining a backup plan for salvation through sin. It is time to kill it. Put it to death before it kills you, your spouse, and your marriage.

For the grace of God that brings salvation has appeared to all men, teaching us that denying ungodliness and wordly lusts, we should live soberly, righteously, and godly in the present age. (Titus 2:11–12)

The same presence and power of God the Holy Spirit, who enabled Jesus Christ to resist every temptation, resides in every Christian. By His power, you can overcome sexual sin. Receive this grace of God and your marriage will never be the same.

REVIEW: How has God brought healing to your relationship by taking away your disgrace?

WATCH VIDEO: REAL MARRIAGE
VIDEO 8: THE PORN PATH

SCRIPTURE REFLECTION

God not only calls us to sexual purity, He sent the Son to die for it and sent the Holy Spirit to make it possible.

Galatians 5:16–24

> I say then: Walk in the Spirit, and you shall not fulfill the lust of the flesh. For the flesh lusts against the Spirit, and the Spirit against the flesh; and these are contrary to one another, so that you do not do the things that you wish. But if you are led by the Spirit, you are not under the law. Now the works of the flesh are evident, which are: adultery, fornication, uncleanness, lewdness, idolatry, sorcery, hatred, contentions, jealousies, outbursts of wrath, selfish ambitions, dissensions, heresies, envy, murderers, drunkenness, revelries, and the like; of which I tell you beforehand, just as I also told you in time past, that those who practice such things will not inherit the kingdom of God. But the fruit of the Spirit is love, joy, peace, longsuffering, kindness, goodness, faithfulness, gentleness, self-control. Against such there is no law. And those who are Christ's have crucified the flesh with its passions and desires.

GROUP DISCUSSION

We are going to meet separately again this week. If you haven't already broken into two groups, this would be a great time to do this.

Men:

Freedom is available if we are willing to submit our lives to Christ as our King and to walk in the Spirit. If we are willing to live in the light and put sin to death, we can experience freedom in our lives and marriages in ways we never thought possible. Take the first step today by being open and honest about areas in which you struggle.

GROUP QUESTIONS

1. Why are porn and lust so deadly to marriages?

2. How does Jesus provide freedom from the bondage of porn addiction and lust?

3. What does it mean to hate sin and kill it?

4. What are you struggling with related to porn and lust?

5. Do you see areas in which you are protecting the sin but hating the circumstances? How does bringing it into the light expose the deadliness of it in your life?

6. Why is it important to find your identity in what Jesus has done rather than define yourself by your sin?

7. How can we call one another to holiness through the gospel that brings life rather than law that will inevitably bring condemnation?

8. Chapter 8 discusses the need to build new ruts in our lives; what does it look like to build new ruts with your wife?

Women:

Lust and porn issues are often issues that men bring into marriage, and rarely are they a result of their dissatisfaction with their wives. But as wives, it is difficult to separate our identity from our husbands' sexual sin. If porn affects our homes, we need to find our identity in Jesus and what He has done as we walk with our husbands toward freedom. Again, be conscientious of respecting your husbands during your group discussion. Also, be willing to confront any pornography or lust issues that arise from the women in the group; these problems are not limited to men only.

GROUP QUESTIONS

1. Why is porn so deadly for marriages?

2. What does it mean for you to find your identity Jesus in practical ways? How can you look to Him for healing the hurt if your husband has a pornography problem?

3. How do you walk with your husband through repentance while hanging on to that identity?

4. What does it look like to trust God through that process?

5. Lust and porn are typically considered a man's problem; however, statistics do not support this notion. What are you struggling with related to porn and lust?

6. How can we call one another to holiness through the gospel that brings life rather than law that will inevitably bring condemnation?

PRAYER

- Pray that we would put sin to death, especially sexual immorality that erodes the intimacy of our marriages.

- Pray for healing in marriages that will be dealing with the confession of sexual sin.

- Pray for freedom through the gospel for those who are in bondage to this sin.

HOMEWORK
INTRODUCTION

This is going to be a tough conversation for most of us, but hiding sin will never lead to life. Be honest with each other, and trust God that He is bigger than your sin.

REFLECT: HUSBAND

1. In what ways are you struggling with lust or porn? What are the triggers that lead you to porn?

2. What does it look like to:
   Be honest with yourself?

   Be honest with God?

   Be honest with your spouse?

   Put this sin to death?

   Submit to the Holy Spirit?

   Practice sexual contentment?

Build new ruts with your wife?

3. If you are willing to kill the porn problem, write down the name of the person you will talk to first for help.

4. At some point this week, read chapter 9 in the book.

REFLECT: WIFE

1. Who does God say you are?

2. In what ways does Jesus give us hope in the face of another's sin and bondage?

3. If you are struggling with porn or lust, what does it look like to:
   Be honest with yourself?

   Be honest with God?

   Be honest with your spouse?

Put this sin to death?

Submit to the Holy Spirit?

Practice sexual contentment?

Build new ruts with your husband?

4. If you have a problem with porn or lust, write down the name of the person you will talk to first to get help.

5. At some point this week, read chapter 9 in the book.

CONNECT

1. If one of you has sexual sin to confess, walk through confession, a plan for repentance and change, and a process for forgiveness.

2. If, by God's grace, the problem of lust and porn does not touch your family, discuss what you can put in place to walk in the Spirit together to keep it out of your marriage.

REFLECT: SINGLE

1. In what ways are you struggling with lust and/or porn?

2. What does it look like to:
   Be honest with yourself?

   Be honest with God?

   Put this sin to death?

   Submit to the Holy Spirit?

   Practice sexual contentment?

   Build new ruts?

3. At some point this week, read chapter 9 in the book.

EXPERIENCE

Take time this week to pray together for your marriage. We have tackled a lot of issues up to this point, and this would be a great time to take what you have learned and discovered to the feet of our Father. You may want to fast together as well. Set aside time to earnestly pray together for what God is doing and thank Him for what He has already done.

SINGLES: Set aside time to pray. Pray for what God is doing in you. Pray for contentment in your singleness, and if you feel lead, pray for your future marriage.

SESSION 9

SELFISH LOVERS & SERVANT LOVERS

INTRODUCTION

In most areas of our life, things become clearer when we take our eyes off ourselves. We are inherently selfish people, but by God's grace we have been shown the glory of our God and Savior to remind us where our eyes should be focused.

The key to renewing your friendship with your spouse and experiencing a real marriage is putting away selfishness and learning to serve one another. Our selfishness often shows up in the little things. Song of Solomon 2:15 refers to such things as "the little foxes that spoil the vines." In a vineyard, there is the potential for beauty, wonder, and life. But, the vineyard must be cultivated, weeds must be pulled, and foxes must be kept out.

What foxes are in your vineyard? Where do you serve yourself rather than your spouse? Every time we act selfishly in our marriage, we let foxes run rampant in our vineyard. It attacks unity and drives us from each other. If we want to see our marriage grow and produce fruit, we need to guard our marriage from selfishness. God wants our marriages to grow in unity as a reflection of the unity He enjoys within the Trinity. To that end, Jesus graciously showed us how to keep foxes at bay. He did so with His life.

In Jesus' time on earth He did not use His position, power, or prestige to be served. Jesus said He "came not to be served, but to serve." He walked in humility, even setting aside His divine privileges to become one of us, making our salvation possible. Think about it. The greatest person who has ever lived was the greatest servant, and He taught us how to be great. "If anyone desires to be first, he shall be last of all and servant of all" (Mark 9:35).

If you want to be great in God's economy, you need to die to yourself and serve others. Jesus demonstrated that having power doesn't mean we have to demand to be served. Don't think of how your spouse can serve you better; think about how you can serve your spouse and meet his or her needs. With Christ's example, we are challenged to rethink what it means to be happy rather than demand that we are served. Maybe happiness comes through serving others and bringing joy to their lives.

Sometimes the things we think will make us the happiest actually end up bringing us the most disappointment because they cost us more relationally than they are worth. This is the challenge of marriage: to be a servant lover. To love your spouse like he or she wants and needs to be loved, emotionally and physically. This gets reflected in every room of your house: in the dining room, the kitchen, the family room, and ultimately, the bedroom.

Husbands and wives live on a continuum from selfish to servant both in and out of the bedroom. If a marriage exists between two selfish people, it will be cold and functional at best. If a marriage exists between a selfish person and a servant, the marriage will be self-centered and abusive. If a marriage exists between two servants, it will be increasingly uniting and satisfying for each of them, both in and out of the bedroom.

REVIEW: As you have prayed for your marriage, how has God breathed new hope into what your marriage could be?

WATCH VIDEO: REAL MARRIAGE
VIDEO 9: SELFISH LOVERS & SERVANT LOVERS

VIDEO RESPONSE

What makes a lover selfish?

SCRIPTURE REFLECTION

Our greatest example of a servant heart and humility is our King and Savior Jesus Christ.

Philippians 2:3–8

> Let nothing be done through selfish ambition or conceit, but in lowliness of mind let each esteem others better than himself. Let each of you look out not only for his own interests, but also for the interests of others. Let this mind be in you which was also in Christ Jesus, who, being in the form of God, did not consider it robbery to be equal with God, but made Himself of no reputation, taking the form of a bondservant, and coming in the likeness of men. And being found in appearance as a man, He humbled Himself and became obedient to the point of death, even the death of the cross.

GROUP DISCUSSION

As we continue on our road to healthy marriages, it is time to check our vineyards and expel the foxes. Sometimes we are blind to the areas of our selfishness and need our community to help us see the holes in our fences. Let us help one another be better image-bearers of our Lord.

GROUP QUESTIONS

1. What are some of the "foxes" that can eat away at the fruitfulness of our marriages? Is there anything you feel you have the right to do or not do, to have or not have?

2. Where is pride evident in your life and marriage?

3. It is often easier for us to be generous and selfless with people other than our spouse. Why do you think that is the case?

4. How does understanding why we are selfish help us to repent and become servants?

5. How has Jesus provided for us the best example of being a servant lover?

6. How does understanding what Christ gave up to serve us help you to be more of a servant to others?

7. How can we apply that to our marriages on a daily basis?

PRAYER

- Pray for a clear understanding of what it means that Jesus humbled Himself to become one of us.

- Pray that we would see the foxes in our vineyards and commit to clearing them out.

- Pray for a renewed sense of serving each other in our marriages.

HOMEWORK
INTRODUCTION

The goal in marriage is to reflect the intimacy and submission that we see in the Trinity. Pride and selfishness are foxes that threaten your marriage. Take time to survey your vineyard, and work together to protect it and cultivate a selfless, servant love for each other. Not only will this have an effect on your relationship, it will also affect your bedroom.

REFLECT: HUSBAND

1. Which of the eight reasons why we are selfish found in chapter 9 resonates with you the most?

2. In your marriage, in what ways are you a selfish lover?

3. Write down ten ways you could be a servant lover to your wife.

4. At some point this week, read chapter 10 in the book.

REFLECT: WIFE

1. Which of the eight reasons why we are selfish resonates with you the most?

2. In your marriage, in what ways are you a selfish lover?

3. Write down ten ways you could be a servant lover to your husband.

4. At some point this week, read chapter 10 in the book.

CONNECT

1. What foxes do you see in your vineyard? Of the nine ways we are selfish lovers, which do you see evidence of in your marriage?

2. How does selfishness affect your intimacy?

3. Share your list of ways you can be a servant lover and add ones that your spouse suggests.

REFLECT: SINGLE

1. Where do you see evidence of selfishness in your life?

2. How would marriage reveal more areas of selfishness?

3. What can you do now to cultivate a pattern of servant-mindedness as a single person?

4. At some point this week, read chapter 10 in the book.

EXPERIENCE

In light of the discussion regarding being servant lovers, this week you will each plan a date night for your spouse. Think about what events, experiences, meals, or places they would enjoy the most, and build an entire day or evening to bless him or her. Think of it as Husband Day or Wife Day. Make it fun, make it memorable, and make it a plan to do it several times a year.

SINGLES: This is your last chance during this study to bless the married couples in your group. Thank you for serving them during this study. As before, this is another opportunity to offer your babysitting services for couples in your group or church. Your offer might be accepted more readily if you are well-known to the family and work in pairs. Don't be offended if parents decline; this could be a great blessing for some families.

SESSION 10

CAN WE _____?

INTRODUCTION

Law produces condemnation and bondage. The gospel produces life and freedom. This is not only true of salvation; it is true in every aspect of our daily lives and especially true in your intimate relationship with your spouse. A healthy sex life and a healthy understanding of sex are essential for a healthy marriage. Learning to talk about sex and ask questions as a couple is important in renewing your marriage and enjoying each other as God intended. With that said, we assume you have plenty of questions when it comes to sex and marriage.

In responding to questions about sex and other behaviors from the church at Corinth, Paul not only taught them what to think, he taught them how to think. Amidst his teaching on sex, Paul said in 1 Corinthians 6:12, "All things are lawful for me, but all things are not helpful. All things are lawful for me, but I will not be brought under the power of any."

This simple taxonomy is brilliantly helpful because it is simultaneously simple enough to remember and broad enough to apply to every sexual question. When it comes to sexual behavior and practices, we can approach them with three questions based on 1 Corinthians 6:12:

Question #1: Is it lawful? With this question we seek to ascertain whether or not something is in violation of the laws of the government in our culture and/or the laws of God in the Scripture.

Question #2: Is it helpful? With this question we seek to ascertain whether or not something pulls a couple together as one or pushes them apart as two. If a sex act includes humiliation, degradation, violation of conscience, pain, or harm, then it is not beneficial for the marriage. If a sex act includes one of the six purposes of sex that we established in chapter 10, it may be helpful:

1. pleasure
2. children
3. oneness
4. knowledge
5. protection
6. comfort

Question #3: Is it enslaving? With this question we seek to ascertain whether or not an act will become obsessive, out of control, or addictive in an unhealthy and concerning way (what the Bible calls slavery). Most people think of slavery as someone being overtaken against their will. But, there is another form of slavery that is even more common: chosen slavery. Chosen slavery is when people freely choose the slave master that rules over them, controls them, and harms them. The most common forms of chosen slavery are freely choosing the abuse of drugs, alcohol, gambling, shopping, food, and sex. While there are many contributing factors, people addicted to these kinds of things are, in fact, slaves who have simply chosen which shackles to put their hands into.

These three questions can be asked of sexual behaviors and practices and give couples a framework for deciding whether certain sexual acts are appropriate for them in their marriage.

REVIEW: Explain how having a servant mentality changes your perspective on your marriage. (LEADERS: be sure that everyone has read this chapter in the book.)

WATCH VIDEO: REAL MARRIAGE
VIDEO 10: CAN WE _____?

VIDEO RESPONSE

In what areas of your life do you see opportunity to apply the process of asking 1) is it lawful, 2) is it helpful, and 3) is it enslaving?

SCRIPTURE REFLECTION

Freedom comes from understanding what Christ has done and receiving His grace. When we receive the gospel in this way, it brings life and joy to our lives and marriage.

> 1 Corinthians 6:12
>
> All things are lawful for me, but all things are not helpful. All things are lawful for me, but I will not be brought under the power of any.

GROUP DISCUSSION

Our marriages can only benefit from learning to submit our lives to God and to receive His grace. Unfortunately we often replace the law (legalistic ways of living and thinking) with a revised Christian version of expectations and rules. Law is law, and learning to navigate questions about sex in light of the gospel and grace will make our marriages stronger and more enjoyable.

GROUP QUESTIONS

1. Where in your life do you feel you have submitted to a version of Christian law (legalism)? What is the product of that law in your life?

2. How does the gospel provide freedom in those areas?

3. What is the difference between experiencing grace and feeling entitled?

4. Why is it important to understand what it means to be a servant lover before we ask the questions of "can we" in our marriages?

5. Our goal is to experience freedom without becoming enslaved. How can we help one another as a community in finding this balance?

PRAYER

- Pray that the couples in your group would experience freedom and new levels of intimacy that glorify God.

- Pray that God would be the God of your marriage beds.

- Thank God for the blessing of pleasure and intimacy.

HOMEWORK
INTRODUCTION

The purpose of this week's session is to create open dialog about your sex life. This should be fun and exciting but can cause anxiety for many couples. The truth is we often don't talk about these things in marriage because we are self-conscious or embarrassed. Take time this week to talk through the apprehension and start the conversation; you will be glad you did.

REFLECT: HUSBAND

1. What would you most like to ask your wife after reading this chapter in the book?

2. What has kept you from talking to her about your sex life?

3. Make a list of ten questions that begin with "Can we _____?"

4. At some point this week, read chapter 11 in the book.

REFLECT: WIFE

1. What would you most like to ask your husband after reading this chapter in the book?

2. What has kept you from talking to him about your sex life?

3. Make a list of ten questions that begin with "Can we _____?"

4. At some point this week, read chapter 11 in the book.

CONNECT

1. How can you both maintain a servant attitude toward each other while talking through your "can we" questions? What does that look like?

2. Discuss what keeps you from having more open conversations about your sex life.

3. Ask each other your "can we" questions, and walk through the threefold process of questioning the lawful, helpful, and enslaving aspects of each.

REFLECT: SINGLE

1. How do the questions of lawful, helpful, and enslaving help you think through decisions in your life?

2. Of what areas in your life can you ask these questions today?

3. At some point this week, read chapter 11 in the book.

EXPERIENCE

This week's experience should be both informative and liberating. Taking into account what we have learned from chapter 9 on being servant lovers, and in light of your Connect conversation about chapter 10's "can we" questions, set aside an evening for a date night at home. Take out all the stops, as if you were preparing to go out on the town. Shower, do your hair, and get dressed up. But stay home.

SINGLES: Take time this week to pray through what it looks like for you to maintain sexual purity as a single person in the service of Christ.

SESSION 11

REVERSE ENGINEERING YOUR LIFE & MARRIAGE

INTRODUCTION

The most important day of your marriage is the last day. Too many couples only put their best energies into the first day. They make sure that the cake, flowers, clothing, and photos are perfect. They put copious amounts of time, money, and energy into the first day. Although a wonderful first day of marriage is important, it's the last day that really counts.

After ten weeks in this study, you may have realized this process is less about getting the marriage you want and more about experiencing the marriage that God your Father wants for you. For some, it may be surprising that Jesus wants you to have a marriage that is more meaningful, more exciting, and more enjoyable than you were willing to settle for. He is a loving Father who wants the best for His children, and so He calls us to experience a marriage that glorifies Him and brings us the most joy.

It is not enough to simply have the passion and principles to finish well on the last day of your marriage. You also need a plan. Marriages start out with passion and over time accrue principles, but apart from a plan, the passion and principles are powerless. You must choose whether you will spend your time making plans or making excuses. Proverbs teaches us that "The plans of the diligent lead surely to plenty, but those of everyone who is hasty, surely to poverty " (21:5). You don't want to be hasty or negligent when it comes to your marriage.

Ten weeks is not going to deliver the marriage you need. However, if you take what you have learned and prayerfully build a plan to honor God and each other in your marriage, you will be on a trajectory toward transformation. The Lord makes this promise: "Commit your work to the Lord, and your thoughts will be established" (Proverbs 16:3). The rest of your marriage is really up to you and your spouse. Take the principles and tools in this book and set in motion a great life together by God's grace and the Holy Spirit's power.

Because if Christ has set you free . . .

Free to turn from idols

Free to be friends again

Free to be a godly husband

Free to be a godly wife

Free to confess and forgive sin

Free from sin and death . . .

Then you are free indeed.

As we submit our lives to Christ and receive the good news of His death and resurrection, our lives will be transformed. The cross is that important, that powerful, and that relevant to your life and marriage. The gospel is not a promise for an easy life, but it is a promise for a transformed and holy life that will experience a greater and eternal joy. Jesus lived the life you should have lived and died the death you should have died so that you can reveal the truth of what He has done through your marriage. He has done this because of His immeasurable love for you and your spouse.

So take hold of the truth and revive your marriage. Real marriage is not only possible; it has already been purchased.

REVIEW: How have you seen the gospel bring freedom rather than bondage as you reflect on last week's study?

WATCH VIDEO: REAL MARRIAGE
VIDEO 11: REVERSE ENGINEERING YOUR LIFE & MARRIAGE

VIDEO RESPONSE

How much time have you spent planning for the future of your marriage and family? Is it more or less than the time you spend planning for your job or other areas of your life? Why do you think you have approached them differently?

SCRIPTURE REFLECTION

Knowing that God has prepared good works for our lives should inspire us to set goals and accomplish all that we can for the kingdom.

Ephesians 2:8–10

For by grace you have been saved through faith, and that not of your-selves; it is the gift of God, not of works, lest anyone should boast. For we are His workmanship, created in Christ Jesus for good works, which God prepared beforehand that we should walk in them.

GROUP DISCUSSION

Our discussion today will focus on the future. Making plans is great, but plans mean little if we never work them to completion. As a community, contending for our marriages includes encouraging one another toward a Christ-centered vision and helping each other walk out that plan.

GROUP QUESTIONS

1. How has your view of what a real marriage is changed over the past ten weeks?

2. Have you ever considered planning out the last day of your marriage in this way? Why or why not?

3. How might this be valuable to your marriage today? Are there areas of tension in your life today that could have been avoided with proper planning?

4. Sometimes "planning" feels like we're not really walking in faith. How do we hold the wisdom of planning and the faith of trusting God in a God-glorifying tension?

5. In light of this chapter in the book, what kinds of questions should we be asking each other to reverse engineer our marriages? Brainstorm categories and questions as a group.

6. How can we help one another implement the plans we come up with this week?

PRAYER

- Pray that God would inspire and direct your plans rather than bless the plans you come up with.

- Pray that what your group has learned over the past ten weeks would take root in your lives and be reflected in marriages that proclaim the gospel.

- Pray that the process of growing in your marriages would never end as you pursue one another and Jesus.

- Pray that the couples in your group would get the marriages they want—the marriages God intended.

HOMEWORK
INTRODUCTION

This week's homework is about the future. As a couple, you are going to take what you learned and put it into an actionable plan as you submit to God and work toward the last day of your marriage.

REFLECT: HUSBAND

1. God is calling you to lead your wife and family. How can you build a plan with her and fulfill that call?

2. What are your top six priorities?

3. Do those priorities align with what God is calling you to do in your life?

4. What is your vision of the last day of your marriage?

REFLECT: WIFE

1. What is God's calling on your life? How can you work with your husband to create a plan for your lives as you both pursue God's calling?

2. What are your top six priorities?

3. Do those priorities align with what God is calling you to do in your life?

4. What is your vision of the last day of your marriage?

CONNECT

1. Share the vision you have for your last day together.

2. When you are done, skip to this week's experience and start reverse engineering your life together.

REFLECT: SINGLE

1. What are your top six priorities?

2. Do those priorities align with what God is calling you to do in your life?

3. What is your vision for your life in five, ten, and twenty years?

EXPERIENCE

You are going to need some time to put together a plan for your marriage. Pick one of two options:

1. Weekend planning getaway: drop the kids off at grandma's or make other arrangements, and spend an entire weekend devoted to working through the reverse engineering questions in Appendix 2.

2. Set up a series of date nights to work through the reverse engineering questions in Appendix 2.

Take your time, work together, and build a plan that you both are excited about. Put the plan in a visible, convenient place so you can refer to it when you make big decisions, plan vacations, or just need to remember what the last day is going to look like.

SINGLES: Review the experience above for couples and follow the same steps. You may need to modify some of the questions to fit your circumstances, but you benefit greatly from reverse engineering your life as a single person. Build your plan, and be ready to adjust it when God brings you a spouse.

APPENDIX 1:

LEADER THOUGHTS

Leaders, use this as a 10,000-foot view of what you are trying to shepherd your people toward each week. This is only a guide, so feel free to follow the leading of the Spirit as each group will be unique. A full leader's guide is available for download at www.realmarriageresources.com.

SESSION 1: NEW MARRIAGE, SAME SPOUSE

Be sure that each couple has at least one copy of the *Real Marriage* book, and that each person in your group has his or her own copy of this participant's guide. Encourage your group to recognize that the next eleven weeks are going to be intense and might feel like a lot of work but that it will be more than worth it in the end.

This first week will focus on setting expectations for the group. If the members of your group are new or unfamiliar to one another, spend more time getting to know one another. Even if your group has been together for a while, it would be good to review the "Safety" segment of the "How to Use This Guide" section at the front of this book. Providing a safe environment will be crucial to honest dialogue and repentance.

Spend some time walking through the elements of this study guide, particularly the homework sections. Explain that the Group section of the guide will be used during your group times together, and the Homework section is intended for personal use after the session. Point out the Reflection homework for the husband, wife, and single person and the Experience section for each week. Remind the group each week to read (or at least skim) the corresponding chapter in the book as well. You should press the husbands particularly to make a commitment to the homework and prep work for the Experiences.

The goal of this week's discussion is to help your people see the source of their unmet expectations as well as understand that the only hope for their marriages will be found in the gospel.

Remind your group of the homework and to read chapter 2 in the book to prepare for next week's session, and to read chapter 1 if they haven't already.

SESSION 2: FRIEND WITH BENEFITS

It is important in this session to stress the biblical view of marriage and friendship so that we don't just see it as good advice but understand that it is a gift from God. This session can be fun and light but should be challenging as well. Challenge couples on question 2 to see where they may be divergent in their views of friendship.

One big idea in this session is the fact that happiness is a by-product of a marriage that glorifies God. God uses marriage to sanctify us and grow us in our walk with Christ. It is more about God than it is about what we want. As the leader of the group, unpack the answers that are given to ensure that everyone understands this idea.

The second big idea is that transformation in our marriages requires us to receive the gospel, not "do more." Doing more is law (legalism) and will lead to condemnation and frustration. Responding to the gospel is grace. We still have to act, but responding to Christ is life-giving and fruitful. If your group does not get this distinction, change will not last—changes that are made will be founded on duty and legalism instead of love and grace.

Remind your group of the homework and to read chapter 3 in the book.

SESSION 3: MEN AND MARRIAGE

First, separate your group by men and women for this session. Remind everyone of the expectations of safety and respect as you all discuss this topic. Each group can meet in a different room or even on a different night if that is what works for your group. Designate one of the women in your group to lead the women's discussion.

Challenge the men to take an honest look at how they are doing as husbands. Remind the men to speak honestly to each other and point out where they see blind spots in each other's lives. Let the men speak freely about areas in which they are struggling, but make sure you get back to the gospel and what Jesus has done to bring freedom.

This would be a great time to check in with the guys to see if they are leading well in planning the Experiences and doing the homework.

For the women's group, be careful not to allow gossip about your husbands. Some women may be married to men who have only recently decided to be a part of a church or even think about taking a spiritual leadership in the family. As a group, focus on ways you can encourage your husbands and spend time in prayer for them.

Remind your group of the homework and to read chapter 4 in the book.

SESSION 4: THE RESPECTFUL WIFE

Again, separate your group by men and women. Remind everyone of the expectations of safety and respect as you all discuss this topic. Each group can meet in a different room or even on a different night if that is what works for your group. Designate one of the women in your group to lead the women's discussion.

Challenge the men to understand that God has given them His daughters to nurture and lead. Their wives are, of course, responsible for their own decisions, actions, thinking, and sin, but as the head of the home, husbands take responsibility for the state of their marriage. Loving their wives in the same way Christ loved the church will transform their marriages. When husbands run to the foot of the cross, their wives will follow if they are not already there.

For the women's discussion, don't allow the group time to become an opportunity to justify sin. Challenge excuses and justification with the expectation of Scripture while showing that Jesus is empathetic to the struggles of life. He cares and gives a way not only to run from sin but to live life to the fullest in His care. The purpose of this session is not to "put women in their place" or to patronize them but to encourage them to live out the callings God has on their lives.

Remind your group of the homework and to read chapter 5 in the book.

SESSION 5: TAKING OUT THE TRASH

The discussion questions in this session are designed to talk about what it means to confess, repent, and forgive. You as the leader should be ready for someone to unload his or her burdens within the group. If this happens, pray, remember the gospel, and don't be afraid to let the community deal with it. It might get messy, but trust the Holy Spirit to work through the people in your group. We don't need sanitary groups, so this might be the best thing to happen to your community. Just make sure that any discussions are honoring to God, and if you have to call a time-out, feel free to do so.

Some people are unwilling to forgive. If you sense resistance from someone in your group, gently remind them of what Jesus did and what He had to forgive. Matthew 6:15 would be a good scripture to read to help the person understand that if we have been forgiven we should be that much more willing to forgive others.

Remind your group of the homework and to read chapter 6 in the book.

SESSION 6: SEX: GROSS, GOD, OR GIFT?

Some individuals in your group may be very uncomfortable talking about sex. It would be good to address that reality at the beginning of the group time. Assure the group that the discussion will not get into specifics or personal experiences, but will focus on the biblical understanding of sex and intimacy.

Most people compartmentalize their thoughts and put faith and sex into separate categories. Challenge your group to submit their view of sex to Scripture. Assure them that doing so does not take the fun and joy out of intimacy. Rather, it will enhance it as we align with the purposes of the Creator.

Remind your group of the homework and to read chapter 7 in the book.

SESSION 7: DISGRACE AND GRACE

This session may bring up delicate issues, and you need to be ready if that is the case. Review Appendix 3 before the meeting to prepare in the event that someone shares an experience with assault or abuse. Two things: One, trust the gospel and the ability of your group to handle even tough issues (but don't let a struggling person leave the group without having the next step for getting help). And two, if you are in over your head, call your pastor or another church staff member as soon as possible. If someone in your group has been an abuse victim and has never sought counseling, go the extra mile to help that person find biblical, professional help. If a crime has been committed or someone is in danger, you will need to call the police. If you are in doubt, err on the side of safety and make the call.

The goal of this discussion is to remind the group that Jesus has taken our shame and cleansed us of our sin and any sin that was done against us. This session serves to remind them of the immense power of the gospel to heal them so that they do not let shame keep them in bondage to things they had no control over. Many people believe the lies associated with abuse experiences. As a leader, you can listen for ideas or thoughts that are in opposition to the gospel and can help replace the lies with God's truth.

The gospel should have a freeing effect on believers. If you sense bondage, pursue further. Offer to stay after the group time to talk with anyone who needs further help.

Remind your group of the homework and to read chapter 8 in the book.

SESSION 8: THE PORN PATH

Separate your group by men and women. Remind everyone of the expectations of safety and respect as you all discuss this sensitive topic. Each group can meet in a different room or even on a different night if that is what works for your group. Designate one of the women in your group to lead the women's discussion.

For the guys, it is time to come clean and be honest about how they are dealing with lust and porn. Remind them that the gospel is bigger than their sin and offers the way to freedom if they are willing to submit themselves to it.

For the women, the biggest issue will be facing the attack on their identity that the sexual sin of their husbands wages on them. Wives need to be reminded of their value and worth in Jesus and encouraged to not let their husbands' sin define them. Women will also need to be willing to discuss any of their own issues with lust or pornography.

Husbands who confess sexual sin will need to confess this to their wives and vice versa. As the leader and as a community, make sure you walk alongside those couples through the process of redemption. Be prepared with suggestions for further help for couples, including biblical, professional counseling and other resources for healing.

Both men and women need to be reminded of the reconciling power of the cross and the truth that freedom from habitual sin is possible when we submit our lives fully to Jesus.

Remind your group of the homework and to read chapter 9 in the book.

SESSION 9: SELFISH LOVERS & SERVANT LOVERS

The challenge this week will be to help couples see how their own pride is contributing to the dissatisfaction in their marriages and help them to humbly come together to build servant-oriented marriages.

Encourage couples to let the other spouse tell them how well they are doing as a servant, not to condemn each other but to help each other grow.

Make the connection to what Jesus has done so that they can see the relevance of the gospel to their daily lives.

Remind your group of the homework and to read chapter 10 in the book.

SESSION 10: CAN WE _____?

While the bulk of the content for this week's chapter is sex, we will spend most of the discussion time on how to navigate questions of what is permissible and beneficial in any area of life. The goal is to learn how to ask the right questions and prepare couples and singles to be able to thoughtfully and biblically assess areas in their life with a few simple questions.

The big idea is that the gospel should bring freedom, joy, and life into one's marriage. Legalism and law always bring condemnation and death. Encourage your group to find freedom through the cross.

This will prepare couples to apply these questions to their sex lives during their Connect time this week.

Remind your group of the homework and to read chapter 11 in the book.

SESSION 11: REVERSE ENGINEERING YOUR LIFE & MARRIAGE

At the beginning of this session, have the group share how they have changed over the past ten weeks. Ask how their perceptions of marriage have changed and how their experiences of marriage are changing. This can provide motivation for completing this final session.

While ten weeks is a good start to seeing transformation in marriages, it can all come to a stop right here if a plan for the future isn't made. Lead your group to make a commitment to finish strong. As the leader, make a note to follow up with the husbands in a week to see how their reverse engineering experience is going.

To close your final group session, spend some extra time praying for the marriages in your group and commit them to Jesus. After all, He is the one who makes healthy marriages possible.

Give a final reminder for your group to do the homework and finish strong.

REVERSE ENGINEERING QUESTIONS

REVERSE ENGINEERING QUESTIONS

The following questions are ones we have used. You are free to add to them and delete them as needed.

STEP #1

Write out no more than seven priorities, and rank them in order of importance (e.g., physical health, spiritual health, marital intimacy, parenting success). We have given you the first four, and we always recommend that they be in this order. The truth is, most people will have a full plate focusing on just these four, and even people with a big plate cannot usually do more than seven things well. For you, this means that anything not on the list has to be cut because it is prohibiting you from pursuing your God-given priorities.

1. Christian

2. Spouse

3. Parent

4. Worker (both paid and unpaid, such as being a stay-at-home mom)

5.

6.

7.

STEP #2

Pick a day for yourself, your family, and your ministry sometime in the future (e.g., two years, five years, ten years) and envision that day. Pick a day that is far enough down the road that you have to work to get there but is not so distant that you cannot see it. Then, answer as many pertinent, specific questions about life on that day as you can reasonably generate. Examples of those questions include:

Spiritual

1. What church will you attend? Will it be a church with strong men leading so that the husband is motivated, engaged, and committed?

2. What criteria will determine what church you choose?

3. How will you serve in that church and be a blessing?

4. How many weeks of the year will you attend services?

5. What group or class will you be involved in to serve and grow?

6. How will you regularly teach your children about Jesus from the Bible?

7. How can you be vitally connected relationally in community with other people in the church, including older people you learn from, peers you walk with, and younger people you are mentoring?

8. What will evangelism and mission to your neighbors and community look like?

9. What will your spouse and children think about Jesus because of you?

10. Who in your spheres of family, friends, coworkers, and neighbors will you have shared the gospel with, seeking their salvation?

11. Husbands, how will you "wash her in the Word"?

Health

1. How much will you weigh?

2. How much will you exercise weekly?

3. What will have changed about your appearance?

4. How many hours of sleep will you average a night?

5. How many times a week will you nap?

6. On which day will you Sabbath?

7. What will your diet be?

8. Other?

Employment

1. What will your job be?

2. How will your work be an act of worship for you unto God?

3. What can you do to become the best employee possible?

4. How will you need to guard your job from consuming your life and overtaking your other higher priorities?

Financial

1. What is your job? Will both spouses be working?

2. Where do you work?

3. How much money do you make?

4. How is your money spent?

5. How is your money saved?

6. How is your money invested?

7. How is your money tithed?

8. What is your insurance, medical, and dental package?

9. Other?

Marriage

1. How often do you pray together?

2. When is your date night?

3. How do you take better care of each other?

4. Why has your love grown?

5. How has your home become a place for unplanned connecting?

6. What brings you together?

7. Other?

Sex

1. What have you and your spouse experimented with?

2. How often are you intimate?

3. What things are different?

4. How have you and your spouse changed physically and sexually?

5. What is different about your bedroom?

6. Other?

Family

1. How many children will you have?

2. How old will your children be?

3. How will they be educated at that time?

4. What special attention will each child need regarding their maturation up to that day?

5. Which family and friends are you closest with as a family?

6. What activities will you allow your children to participate in and how will you manage all the time required for them?

7. Who will be the primary caregiver of your child(ren)?

8. Other?

Housing/Living

1. Where will you live?

2. How will the home be laid out (e.g., yard, deck, hot tub, bedrooms, bathrooms, garage, family room, dining space, kitchen, etc.)?

3. How will you use your home for your family, hospitality, and ministry?

4. How long is your commute?

5. How can you redeem your commute by making calls, listening to Bible teaching, and so on?

6. What vehicle will you drive?

7. What are the features of your home (e.g., parking for guests, square footage, size of yard, home library, hardwood floors, air conditioning)?

8. What furniture and appliances will you have gotten rid of or acquired?

9. Other?

Bedroom

1. What will your bedroom be like?

2. How will your bedroom be romantic and a private oasis to connect?

3. Will you have a TV in your bedroom? (If you have a TV, keep it separate and not at the foot of your bed.)

4. Will you have a private master bath?

5. Will you have a lock on your bedroom door for privacy if you have children?

6. Will you keep all your work (e.g., computers, projects, desk) out of your bedroom?

Technology

1. How will you use technology but not allow it to rule your life?

2. When will you agree to have the phone and computer off (e.g., dinner time, while in your bedroom, on date night)?

Extended Family

1. Which close relatives are not living?

2. What is your relationship like with each close family member (e.g., mom, dad, brother, sister, grandparent)?

3. How will you include or not include your extended family in vacations and holidays?

4. What has changed with your extended family?

5. Other?

Friends

1. How will you be better friends to each other?

2. Who are your closest friends?

3. Which people have you dropped as friends?

4. What things do you do with your friends?

5. Who no longer has your direct phone number and/or email?

6. Other?

Learning

1. What areas have you studied deeply?

2. How many books have you read by that date? What are some of the titles?

3. What other learning experiences have shaped you (e.g., conferences, mentors, spiritual disciplines)?

4. How much time do you spend reading each day?

5. Other?

Daily Habits

1. How will you pray alone and together as a couple each day?

2. How will you ensure you eat at least one meal together nearly every day?

3. What will your daily Bible reading be?

Weekly Routine

1. What will your ideal week look like?

2. What will your weekly Sabbath day look like? What will you do to relax as a family and have fun together?

3. What weekly routines will provide anchors to your schedule (e.g., family movie night, family breakfast before school)?

4. What small group or class will you be in together at your church to grow and serve?

Weekly Date Night

1. What will your weekly date night look like? Where will you go? What will you do? How will you connect?

2. If you have kids, how will you get childcare for date night (e.g., pay a babysitter, ask relatives, co-op with other families where you rotate who takes the kids each week, finding a single in the church who will volunteer because he/she wants to learn about marriage and kids)?

Quarterly Getaway

1. Will you go away roughly once a quarter for at least one night together? What will you do together?

2. What/where sounds fun and romantic to connect?

STEP #3: MAKING CHANGES

Changes

1. What three things do you hope have changed with your spouse? Yourself? Your ministry? Your family? Your job?

2. What top three emotion-, time-, and energy-wasters do you need to drop immediately?

3. What three changes in your life would make the biggest difference?

4. What three things do you need the most (e.g., different car, gym membership, computer, home office, cell phone, high-speed wi-fi at home)?

5. What obstacles are keeping you from living by your convictions (e.g., a cluttered house, no budget, lack of prayer time)?

People

1. List the people who take but don't give toward a friendship, and determine if you are to continue serving them, back off your involvement in their lives, or simply make them take care of themselves.

2. Who do you need to distance yourself from because they are taking time, money, and/or energy away from your first priorities?

Handing Off

1. List all the things you can hand off to someone else (e.g., ordering groceries online and having them delivered, mowing your lawn, doing your taxes, household projects, watching kids, running errands, outsourcing dry cleaning and ironing, scheduling appointments, answering your phone).

HELPING VICTIMS OF ABUSE OR ASSAULT

The suggestions in this appendix are from Justin and Lindsey Holcomb, authors of *Rid of My Disgrace: Hope and Healing for Sexual Assault Victims*.

WAYS YOU CAN HELP VICTIMS

1. Listen. Don't be judgmental. Research has proven that the only social reactions related to better adjustment for victims were being believed and being listened to by others.

2. Let them know the assault(s) was not their fault.

3. Let them know they did what was necessary to prevent further harm.

4. Reassure them that they are cared for and loved.

5. Be patient. Remember, it will take them some time to deal with the crime.

6. Encourage sexual assault victims to seek medical attention.

7. Empower victims. Don't tell them what they should do or make decisions on their behalf, but present the options and help them think through them.

8. Encourage them to talk about the assault(s) with an advocate, a pastor, a mental health professional, a law-enforcement officer, or someone they trust.

9. Let them know they do not have to manage this crisis alone.

10. Remember that sexual assault victims have different needs (what may have been beneficial for one person might not work for another).

11. Remember not to ask probing questions about the assault. Probing questions can cause revictimization. Follow the victim's lead and listen.

PRACTICAL WISDOM FOR SPOUSES

If you are a husband or wife who is walking with your spouse through the effects of sexual assault, here are some suggestions for how to best care for them.

1. Don't minimize, deny, or blame him/her for what happened.

2. Listen to his/her experience and do not ask probing questions about the assault. Let him/her divulge what they want to when they want to. Because sexual assault is a form of victimization that is particularly stigmatized, many victims suffer in silence, which only intensifies their distress and disgrace. There appears to be a societal impulse to blame traumatized individuals for their suffering. Research findings suggest that blaming victims is not only wrong but also contributes to the vicious cycle of traumatization. Victims experiencing negative social reactions have poorer adjustment. Research has proven that the only social reactions related to better adjustment for victims are being believed and being listened to by others.

3. Challenge the myths and misconceptions that promote self-blame. Self-blaming is a common behavior among victims. As a coping technique and to make sense of the assault, victims make attributions for why the assault occurred. Self-blame is associated with more distress and poorer adjustment. Unchallenged sexual assault myths perpetuate feelings of guilt, shame, and self-blaming tendencies for victims. Refusal to accept these myths may help victims to assign different meaning to the experience instead of society's stereotypical ideas regarding sexual assault.

4. Learn what to say and what not to say. Reflect theologically when he/she is ready. Connect the grace of the gospel to the disgrace of sexual assault and the specific effects connected to it (denial, distorted self-image, shame, guilt, anger, and despair). It is important to address the effects of sexual assault with the biblical message of grace and redemption. Jesus responds to victims' pain and past. The message of the gospel redeems what has been destroyed and applies grace to disgrace.

5. Fight against the lies for him/her. Communicate frequently this message: "What happened to you was not your fault. You are not to blame. You did not deserve it. You did not ask for this. You should not be silenced. You are not worthless. You do not have to pretend like nothing happened. Nobody had the right to violate you. You are not responsible for what happened to you. You are not damaged goods. You were supposed to be treated with dignity and respect. You were the victim of assault, and it was wrong. You were sinned against. Despite all the pain, healing *can* happen, and there *is* hope" (*Rid of My Disgrace*, page 15, emphasis in original).

6. Be sure to take care of yourself as a support person, so you can be healthy in your care-giving role.

7. Encourage him/her to tell a friend or friends he/she trusts. It is a good idea for victims to have a broad support base as it can be exhausting for the supporting spouse if he/she is the only one involved. The supporting spouse won't always be available to talk and at times it can be easier for a victim to talk to someone of the same sex about certain dimensions of an assault.

8. Don't ever pressure or whine for sex or physical intimacy.

DATE NIGHT TIPS

1. Parents, if you cannot afford a sitter, is there a way to set up a rotation with other families to take turns each week watching kids for date night? If you have four families, you can get a date night three times a month.

2. Husbands, when is your date night? Your wife needs it. You do too. We've enjoyed Friday date nights for about twenty years.

3. Husbands, don't waste every date night at a movie where you can't talk. Use the time to visit with your wife, draw her out, and study her like you do the Bible.

4. Plan out your date nights. Ask your spouse in advance what sounds good, ask for options, make a plan, and he/she will be thankful.

5. Date night killers: no plan, selfishness, laziness, letting technology keep interrupting, and doing the same old predictable thing.

6. Time with other couples now and then is OK, but if most date nights involve other people, there is likely an intimacy disconnect in the marriage.

7. Dads, moms who stay home all day with the kids need to get dressed up, be taken out, and have some adult conversation with their husbands.

8. Husbands, what can you do to find some creative ways to make date night fun and endearing even on a tight budget?

9. Husbands, what can you start doing days or hours before date night to build the expectation of connection with your wife? Flowers, cards, calls, texts?

10. When life gets crazy, the kids are sick, and so on, is there any way to sneak in a bit of a date night at home with perhaps a soak in the tub together or a glass of wine after the kids go to sleep?

11. Sometimes sending the kids out to someone's house and having a date night at home can be cheap and fun if planned right.

12. Men, you don't pursue a woman to marry her then stop pursuing her. You pursue a woman to marry her and pursue her with more passion and creativity than ever. How's it going, husbands?

13. Men, you don't need to understand women. You will be doing better than most to understand one woman. Date nights are for asking inviting questions, listening, and learning about her. It's also a night to open up and let her do the same. Engage in conversation.

14. Men, if you don't date your wife, someone else may eventually volunteer for the job.

15. Ladies, sometimes it's a great gift to go into your husband's world for a date night by doing something like putting on a jersey, going to a game, and eating a hot dog. His love language may just be hot dog.

16. Men, here are some date night tips—find a shirt with buttons, try two eyebrows instead of one for a change, find a breath mint or twenty, show up with a gift, don't ogle other women, and go to a restaurant that does not have a spork.

17. Sometimes the best date night is date breakfast, date lunch, or to pick up your spouse from work for a surprise hour at a hotel.

18. If your spouse likes board games, a fun date night is finding a nice spot to be (like the beach) with a beverage of choice and time to play and chat.

19. Sometimes takeout is fun, and a drive somewhere more private can turn it into a picnic or adventure.

20. A nice, relaxing candlelight massage is always a good date night, especially if your spouse is high touch.

21. Every once in a while you just have to have a redneck date night and go bowling, play pool, or throw darts.

22. Plan in advance for some big events like concerts, comedians, plays, cirque show, and so on. Who is coming to town? What would be fun?

23. Men, take your wife shopping. Yes, shopping at a place that does not also sell carburetors or fishing supplies. Patiently help her pick things out, watch her try them on, flatter her with comments, and spend some money.

24. Sometimes it is fun to go on an old memorable date again. Retrace a first date, relive the memory, and recollect what God has done since then.

25. A few times a year, a couple needs an overnight date. Even if it's just one night away with a discount room on Priceline, dinner out, and time to chill.

26. If you have no idea what to talk about on date night, take turns picking a book, each read a chapter a week, and discuss what you learned on date night to kick-start conversation.

27. Husbands, have you ever just asked your wife what things she's always wanted to do but never told you? You can plan some epic date nights off that list.

28. It's always a good idea to take a camera on date night, snap some memorable photos, and revisit them sometimes to have a laugh and celebrate the times you've enjoyed.

29. If money is tight for date night, ask for gift cards to places you like for birthday and holiday presents from family and friends. Then, after you use them, send them a thank-you note so they know what a blessing it was.

"GETTING TO KNOW YOUR SPOUSE" QUESTIONNAIRE

The following questions are many of the same ones we use for the pre-marital counseling at our church as an assignment for those wanting to be married. In offering them we are not expecting anyone to go through them all, or worse still, to use them like an interrogation. Instead, over the course of many conversations, it might be interesting to comb through the questions and ask your spouse some of the more curious ones you stumble across and then listen respectfully to see what you can learn.

SPIRITUAL BACKGROUND

1. What is the gospel?

2. Who is Jesus?

3. Do you consider yourself a Christian? Why?

4. What role do you want to see Jesus playing in your marriage?

5. What kind of religious upbringing did you have?

6. How did your parents influence your beliefs of God?

7. List ways that your family exhibited a faith or belief in God (prayer before meals, reading the Bible together, etc.).

8. Have you been baptized? When?

9. How do you practice spiritual disciplines (prayer, Bible reading, attend church, etc.)?

10. What is sin?

11. What sins do you struggle with most frequently?

12. How pleased are you with your spiritual life together, including praying, attending church, being in a Bible study small group, and serving God?

13. How would you describe your personal journey as a Christian?

14. How strong do you think your faith is?

15. What have been the highlights of your relationship with Christ and of your church or ministry involvement?

16. What are the main ways you've seen God active in and through you?

17. What are some special times when you have seen God provide for you?

18. When were some times when you felt that you were not walking with God very closely? Why do you think that happened?

19. What are some areas in which you want to see God work in your life?

AUTHORITY FIGURES

1. As you look at your past, how have you traditionally responded to authority (for example, parents, employers, teachers, coaches, pastors)?

2. How have you responded to Christ's authority in your life?

3. How do you think the way you respond to authority will affect your relationship with your future spouse?

4. As a wife, do you respect your husband, enable him, or disrespect him?

5. As a husband, do you lead lovingly or abdicate leadership to your wife?

FAMILY HISTORY

1. Were your parents divorced? If so, did they remarry? If so, which parent got custody of you?

2. How would you describe your parents' marriage?

3. Choose three to five adjectives to describe your relationship with your father and why you chose them.

4. Choose three to five adjectives to describe your relationship with your mother and why you chose them.

5. In what ways are you like your parents?

6. In what ways are you different?

7. In what ways do you want to emulate your parents' relationship?

8. What are the ways you do not want to emulate their relationship?

9. Are there any unresolved issues between you and your parents? Explain.

10. How well do you think you have left your parents to unite as a new family with your spouse?

11. What were your parents' expectations of you at school, work, or in sports?

12. What kind of prejudices do your parents have, if any?

13. What traditions do you want to pass on to your family? What traditions do you not want to pass on to your family?

14. In what ways did you rebel against your parents?

15. What kind of neighborhood did you grow up in?

16. Who worked in your family (mom, dad, both)?

17. Would you describe your family as poor, middle class, fairly affluent, wealthy, rich?

18. Who disciplined you? Did your parents agree on discipline?

19. Was your home open (frequent visitors and activities), closed (more structured meals, etc., and less visitors coming and going) or even random (no set schedule, people coming and going, even dangerous lack of oversight)?

20. How expressive was your family in word and deed?

21. How did your family address sensitive subjects?

22. Who made the rules? Who enforced the rules?

23. What was the standard of living in your home?

24. How did your family view finances and debt?

25. Who controlled the money?

26. Who was in charge? Who made the decisions?

27. How did your father divide his time between work and family? Was it balanced?

28. How did you learn about sex?

29. How did your family view work?

30. How did your family view recreation?

31. How did your family view education?

32. How did your family view politics?

33. How did your parents divide household responsibilities?

34. What values held priority in your home?

35. What things did your family do for recreation?

36. What did your family do for vacations?

37. How did your family handle holidays?

38. How did your family handle birthdays?

39. What was it like to be sick in your home?

40. How did your family manage the television, phone, computer, and other technology?

41. Did your family eat meals together?

42. What were the bedtime routines in your home?

43. How did your family relate to, for example, grandparents, aunts, uncles, cousins?

44. What were the highlights of your family?

45. What were the lowlights of your family?

46. How much privacy were you given at home?

47. How much freedom and independence were you given?

48. How many times did you move growing up?

49. Was your family public or private about their struggles and frustrations?

OTHER RELATIONSHIPS

1. How did you choose your friends?

2. How long do most of your friendships last? Why?

3. If you have had any long, enduring friendships, what has kept them going? If not, what are some reasons?

4. Have you been damaged by any of these relationships? How? If yes, how can God help you reverse the damage?

5. Is there any history of violence or sexual abuse in your past relationships?

6. Have you been previously married or engaged? If so, please explain.

7. Have you ever had a homosexual or bisexual experience? If so, please explain.

WORK AND CAREER

1. On a scale of 1 to 10 (1 being bad, 10 being good) how would you rate your work ethic? Why?

2. How many jobs have you held in the past five years? Why did you change jobs (if you did)?

3. At what age did you begin working? Why?

FINANCES

1. How much financial debt do you have, including credit cards, car payments, school loans, mortgage? Please list all debt.

2. What are your attitudes and beliefs regarding money?

3. Have you ever declared bankruptcy?

4. Do you believe your giving to God is adequate?

5. Do you believe you need to grow in issues related to stewarding your finances? What should you do to accomplish that?

COUPLE RELATIONSHIP

1. Have you been engaged before? Explain.

2. What do your parents, other family members, and friends think of your relationship? Does anyone disapprove?

3. What are your character strengths? Weaknesses?

4. As a couple, what are the strengths of your relationship?

5. As a couple, in what areas do you need to grow in your relationship?

6. How well do you make decisions together? How could you improve this area of your marriage?

7. What has been most difficult about marriage? Why? How could your spouse help you?

8. What are five reasons you married your spouse?

9. Are there any areas of concerns you have about him or her? (Some areas of concern might be lack of common interests, frequent arguments, or anger concerns.)

10. Has he or she ever pushed you, grabbed you, yelled at you, threatened you, or demonstrated other abusive behaviors?

11. Have you discussed having children? How many? When? Will she work after you have children?

12. What attracted you to each other?

13. What are some of the favorite things you've done together?

OTHER PERSONAL QUESTIONS

1. Have you ever been arrested for a crime? When?

2. Have you ever used any drugs? When was the last time?

3. Have you ever used alcohol to excess? Explain.

4. Have you ever experienced any compulsions or addictions (food, drugs, alcohol)?

5. Is there any history of chemical dependency or addiction in your family?

6. Have you ever experienced abuse (sexual, mental, emotional, physical)? Explain.

7. Have you experienced an eating disorder?

8. How is your current physical and mental health?

9. Have you ever been clinically diagnosed with a mental illness including dissociative, depressed, borderline, bipolar I or II, panic or anxiety disorder?

10. Is there any history of mental illness in your family?

11. Have you received professional counseling (psychologist, psychiatrist) or lay counseling through a church? When and for what reasons?

12. Have you ever experienced problems with anger? Describe.

13. Have you ever attempted suicide or do you have suicidal thoughts? Explain.

SEXUAL HISTORY (PLEASE EXPLAIN YOUR ANSWERS.)

1. What is your complete sexual history in addition to your spouse?

2. **Women:** Have you been pregnant before? Do you have any children from a previous relationship?

3. **Men:** Have you gotten anyone pregnant before? Do you have any children from a previous relationship?

4. Have you ever been diagnosed with a sexually transmitted disease?

5. If you have been sexually active in the past, have you been tested for STDs?

6. Is there any history of violence or sexual abuse in your past or current relationship?

7. Have you had any sexual contact with anyone else during your current relationship?

8. Have you ever experienced a same-sex attraction?

9. What is your experience with pornography? Explain: when, for how long, and the last time you viewed it.

10. Are you currently using pornography at all? Explain.

11. Have you experienced ongoing guilt and shame from past sexual sins?

12. Have you been completely honest in answering these questions? Are you withholding anything or keeping something secret? It might seem too hard to tell this information, but lying to your spouse only delays the pain and keeps sin between you, causing division.